Creative Play
for your toddler

Steiner Waldorf expertise
and toy projects for 2–4s

Christopher Clouder and Janni Nicol

An Hachette UK Company
www.hachette.co.uk

First published in Great Britain in 2008 by Gaia,
a division of Octopus Publishing Group Ltd
Endeavour House, 189 Shaftesbury Avenue, London WC2H 8JY
www.octopusbooks.co.uk
www.octopusbooksusa.com

This edition published in 2014

Distributed in the US by Hachette Book Group USA
237 Park Avenue, New York NY 10017 USA

Distributed in Canada by Canadian Manda Group
165 Dufferin Street, Toronto, Ontario, Canada M6K 3H6

ISBN 978-1-85675-351-7

A CIP catalogue record for this book is available from the British Library.

Printed and bound in China

10 9 8 7 6 5 4 3 2 1

Safety notes

The toys in this book have been designed for play with toddlers from
two to four years of age and should be made with due care and
attention. All yarn should be of the kind that does not shed fibres and,
when used for hair, must be stitched on well and tied tightly. All wood
must be seasoned before use (by air- or kiln-drying the cut wood) to
avoid cracking and splitting. Rough or sharp edges on wooden toys
must be sanded smooth. If finishing wood with an oil, use one that will
cause no harm if put in the mouth, such as boiled linseed oil or olive oil.
Check toys periodically for general wear and tear, particularly those with
loose or small parts.

Disclaimer

The publisher cannot accept any legal responsibility or liability for
accidents or damage arising from the use of any items mentioned in this
book or in the carrying out of any of the projects.

Every effort has been made to trace copyright holders of extracts
reproduced in this book. The publisher apologizes for any errors or
omissions and would be grateful if notified of any corrections that
should be incorporated in future reprints or editions of this book.

To our respective children – Emma,
Malinda, Leoma and Kether; Emma
and Alexandra – for their inspiration.

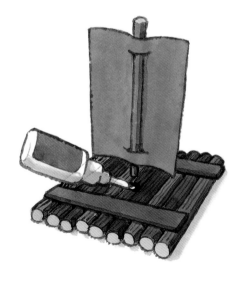

Contents

Introduction

Play is vital to being human and without it we would be much diminished. Although we cannot define precisely what play is, we do know that it has a great value in itself and is essential for our physical, emotional and mental health, regardless of its other practical and utilitarian ends. Play is also a time when there are no goals beyond the activity itself.

Learning through play

Play is a learning activity, through which we first experience cooperation, risk and creativity and begin to discover the physical laws and structure of the world. Play helps our cognitive and kinetic development, and enhances our problem-solving abilities, aesthetic sensitivity and linguistic skills. It teaches us to manage our frustrations and joys, and strengthens our sense of purpose and determination. It encourages self-motivation, helps us find our individual personality and facilitates empathy for others. Play brings together head, hand and heart. It is fundamental to each and every one of us and, although it may change as we mature, it never completely disappears from our lives.

In Steiner Waldorf early childhood centres (see page 9), play is seen as a foundation for later learning. To appreciate the grounds on which such an education is founded, it is worth considering a number of views on childhood through history.

Space to learn

Jean-Jacques Rousseau (1712–1778) introduced the idea of the 'social contract', a process involving various stages through which an individual develops into a member of a community. According to Rousseau, each developmental stage requires an appropriate way of teaching and, because every person is different, learning should also aim to accommodate the individual's development. The educator's role is one of guidance but should not be authoritarian. Rousseau maintained that children differ from adults in that they are innocent, sensitive and vulnerable, yet also have a right to freedom and happiness. They have an inner urge to be active, which lies at the root of their incipient curiosity. Learning is a direct consequence of physical activity, so children need to move in order to learn and are entitled to have the space in which to do so.

Johann Heinrich Pestalozzi (1746–1827) took up these ideas in a practical way at the beginning of the 19th century, founding schools in which a child's own motivation was paramount: each child was encouraged to follow his own questions and find his own answers. Pestalozzi felt that cognitive development was only one side of the personality and that it was important for the whole child to be engaged. His emphasis was on work and not play, however: 'The important thing in good upbringing is that the child should be prepared for his own circle; he must learn to know and to do things that will bring him bread to still his hunger and peace and content to his heart.' There was to be no corporal punishment and every child was to be approached with love on the grounds that maternal love is a manifestation of a greater divine love that keeps us from 'complete selfishness'.

A child's environment

It was Friedrich Froebel (1782–1852) who first used the word 'kindergarten' to refer to a place of play for children, where they were encouraged to play out of their own nature and in a suitable environment. The *garten* metaphor underlines the balance between nature and child development with an emphasis on the qualities of freedom and joy. Interestingly, when we, as adults, think back to our own childhood, the first remembered image of playing is often one of being active in natural surroundings. Froebel's institutions were intended to cultivate family life and provide parents with appropriate guidance. Play equated closely with educational aims in helping the child integrate his experiences. Froebel, like Rousseau, saw children as naturally good – a goodness that could be built upon through nurture.

Maria Montessori (1870–1952) placed her emphasis on the relevance of sense development – first feel, then learn. According to Montessori, there are multiple ways in which a child can learn and each child needs addressing in his own particular way. The child is not a blank slate or empty barrel but has the inherent capacity to discover for himself and is deeply influenced by everything around him. In her book, *The Absorbent Mind*, she wrote: 'The child has a different relation to his environment from ours. Adults admire their environment; they can remember it and think about it; but the child absorbs it. The things he sees are not just remembered; they form part of his soul. He incarnates in himself all the world about him that his eyes see and his ears hear. In us the same things produce no changes, but the child is transformed by them.' Montessori was not, however, promoting creativity but rather independence and

autonomy. Elsewhere, when writing about the imagination of children, she stated: 'It is we that imagine not they; they believe, they do not imagine. Credulity is, indeed, a characteristic of immature minds, which lack experience and knowledge of realities.' From this viewpoint, play is primarily instrumental in building up other faculties and skills.

Rudolf Steiner (1861–1925) recognized the importance of free play and imagination in the context of the developing child and this is now

central to all practice in Steiner Waldorf early childhood centres. The idea is that children have predispositions and gifts that, if fostered by the playgroup or kindergarten, will enable the child to develop into a confident, responsible and free individual. An extended childhood provides an excellent foundation for this development. Finding their own internal balance through play eventually equips children for adulthood, enabling them to reach their full potential in the world.

Creative play in the home

This book shows how you can bring Steiner's theories on early childhood to your two- to four-year-olds. By observing your child and allowing your natural feelings of care to guide you, you can help your child to experience childhood to the full. As well as enjoying free space, children also need

to feel embraced. It is, therefore, important to establish a framework of sorts, within which play is organized. Daily events should be habitual, with different types of play having a recognizable beginning and ending. These should be rhythmical and repetitive, to give the child boundaries and a sense of structure. For example, using a song or finger game to start and conclude playtime gives the child a sense of appropriateness and self-control. Meals or snacks can also provide a homely and natural framework for play. Such a structure is essential if a child is to engage fully his social-emotional, kinetic and creative development. A secure atmosphere helps build a growing child's confidence to enter new worlds.

Each child has the right to daydream and, for toddlers especially, healthy play needs the counterbalance of rest. In affluent societies, there is a steadily increasing bombardment from different media, over-stimulation from electronic devices and a fashion for unceasing entertainment. The toddler is susceptible to this chaos of multiple impressions and needs help in finding his own alternative space in order to come to terms with it all. Our inner resources need strengthening to enable us to cope with the intense demands from the outside world and these resources develop naturally in the years before we begin formal learning. Give your child space to breathe for the sake of his mental and emotional wellbeing.

Playing simple games with your child will help him to communicate with you. From 18 months a child's vocabulary increases exponentially and by two years of age his vocabulary includes a mix of verbs and adjectives. However, facial expressions, movement, behaviour and gestures are still vital forms of communication and can, in certain ways, speak louder than words.

From about 22 months a child can very creatively connect mental pictures, whereas previously these were impressions that stood apart from each other. Connection words and phrases, such as 'as well', 'with' and 'together', appear in his speaking and influence how he plays. New connections are made and your child will express and develop these further through play. You can aid this acquisition process by speaking clearly and directly and avoiding inconsequential chatter. Enjoy his words as if they are new to you, too. It is also beneficial to encourage movement in play. This helps your child's language formation in that the development of networks in the brain is, to a large extent, influenced by how he moves at this early age.

The right pace and environment

You should not push your child, but allow him to follow his own mental processes as they emerge. If his development is to be healthy, he needs time to grow towards thought. The importance of this is underlined again and again by Steiner. In his book, *Extending Practical Medicine*, he states: 'It is of the utmost importance to know that the human being's ordinary forces of thinking are refined form and thinking forces. A spiritual element reveals itself in the form and growth of the human organism. For this spiritual element then appears during the course of later life as the spiritual power of thought.'

The child is still growing and vulnerable and should not be pushed into abstraction and formalization of experience at this stage but rather, with your help and understanding, should enjoy, explore and fully enter the experiences as he encounters them. His thinking is still bound up with his body and its forces of growth, which accounts for its liveliness and freshness. You need to respect this wisdom of nature and allow your child's development to take its own course, strengthening it rather than trying to supplant it with a premature way of thought. It is, after all, the foundation on which our adult logic finally rests. Abstract thought comes in its own good time if we can trust the nature of childhood.

For a child to develop healthily, his home and care settings have to be mutually supportive. The better the understanding of responsible adults, the more positive the situation for the child. Warmth, calmness, interest, gentleness, rhythm, humour and empathy all allay the anxieties of growing into an individual who, in due course, will inevitably be faced with far greater demands and choices. The way we receive our children into the world can give them resources that last a lifetime and in turn provide parenting skills for future generations. This was expressed concisely in the report produced in 1981 by Sweden's Family Aid Commission: 'Basic to a good society is that children are welcome, are given a good environment during childhood and are the concern of the whole society. Children have a right to secure living conditions that enhance their development. Pre-school has an important function in children's lives. It offers a comprehensive programme and is the source of stimulation in the children's development. It gives them a chance to meet other children and adults and to be part of an experience of fellowship and friendship. It is a complement to the upbringing a child gets at home.'

We show our welcome, therefore, by taking a child's play seriously, either at home or in an early years' setting and, by doing so, we show the child that we take him seriously, too.

Self

Self

Up to about the end of her second year, a child lives in the eternal present. Then, together with a rudimentary use of grammar in language, come new concepts of time. Sentences appear that suggest a future and a past, and this shows that the child's mind is able to make representations. In other words, she can conceive of something not present, such as an event that has recently occurred.

Awakening consciousness

From three-quarters of the way through her second year until the start of her third year, a child develops the ability to combine these representations. She can ask 'if' questions about someone not present and can respond to 'or' questions like: 'Would you like to drink water or milk?' although neither are visible at that moment. She can understand the word 'self': a sense grows of the nearby future and out of this derives an understanding of identity. The child realizes that she is the same self as she was a little while ago and as she will be in the immediate future. This is a momentous moment.

As a child's 'I' becomes conscious, at about three years old, her relationship to the sensory world is also transformed. She is no longer just subject to feelings of wanting or not wanting, which originate in bodily desires and needs, but can now begin to respond in a more sympathetic manner. The power of fantasy awakens, and if an inanimate object falls over the child may describe it as being tired and needing to sleep; branches blowing in the wind may 'wave' at the child. The forces that engaged in building up her body – developing the senses, pushing out the milk teeth, enabling standing up and walking, early language acquisition and the

formation of the brain – are, from two and a half years onwards, gradually oriented to other goals. The child's body has found its definitive form and she is increasingly alert.

The growth of the child's consciousness can be observed through play and the child's wish to exercise her new thinking capabilities: she seeks her own path of development through doing. This phase can be misinterpreted and undermined by adults who assume the child is ready for a purely cognitive form of learning. In fact, the process is ongoing and the body still has a long way to go to maturity. The child naturally balances the demands of her developing sense organs and those of her expanding consciousness, which is why a young child needs so much sleep. She needs us to respect this delicate condition and not to destabilize her with inappropriate educational burdens.

The rhythms of life

Rudolf Steiner differentiated between four dimensions, or aspects, of human beings – the physical body, etheric body, astral body and the 'I' or ego (see page 14). These aspects all have developmental rhythms, perceived most easily as we pass through childhood and adolescence. The

more apparent physical changes are symptomatic of deeper changes. We cross certain thresholds every seven years, the first being the change of teeth when we lose our milk teeth, the second the bumpy path through adolescence.

Our physical body prepares itself in the womb and is born, so to speak, at the moment of our birth. In this context the word 'born' is used to suggest a freeing up and greater independence. Our etheric body (life forces) matures throughout the first seven-year period and, in turn, has its own birth at around seven years of age, just as our astral body (emotional and behavioural traits) is born at around 14 and our 'I' or ego fully appears at 21.

The transformation and awareness of self at around three years old has a fundamental connection to the life rhythms of the etheric aspect. Children delight and thrive on repetition, because, paradoxically, repetitiveness strengthens identity and helps to develop the capacities needed to deal

Steiner's four dimensions

Our physical body is the structure that separates us from others, within the space that only we can occupy. In this we share an attribute with the mineral kingdom, plants, animals and other people. This body undergoes constant transformation throughout our lives, most especially when we are young. The network of forces that keeps us alive and drives the process of biological change (again in common with the plants and animals) is the 'etheric body'. This includes the life functions, such as breathing, biochemical processes and regeneration, all of which are connected to temporality. If our etheric body were to leave our physical body there would only be lifeless material left behind. The 'astral body' refers to our emotional and behavioural traits in thinking, feeling and willing. It embodies our sympathies and antipathies, our wishes and desires and our mobility. It is a vehicle of consciousness through which we become aware of joy and sorrow, pain and enthusiasm, memories and relationships. Finally there is our 'I', or 'ego', where our intentions, goals and purposes reside. This is where we can become visible as a personality in what we do and in the life choices that we make. It delineates our identity, encompasses our spiritual nature and is the part of us that is immortal.

with our freedom as individuals. The most recent neurobiological research, as summarized by J. Chilton Pearce in *Evolution's End*, bears this out: 'Children want to hear the same story over and over again, not to "learn" it – most children remember a story after one hearing – but because repetition causes the interweaving neural fields involved in the image-flow to myelinate… Thus, the more stories and their repetitions, the more neural fields and connections are brought into play. The stronger and more permanent the capacity for visual-verbal interaction grows, the more powerful conceptualization, imagination and attentiveness become.' Nursery rhymes, fairy stories and finger games all have repetitive and ritualized elements that children do not find at all boring and that help them anchor into themselves with confidence. In echoing the etheric in our actions with the child, we are contributing to her long-term health and allowing her to express her feelings through play.

Being ourselves

Conscious memories usually begin when we say 'I' to ourselves and are closely intertwined with who we are or who we think we are. Being able to say 'I' is at first a joyful experience, which later leads to questions and doubt. Our sense of identity is ever evolving, in reality never a fixed definition. We can help our children with their future struggles with fluid and interacting identities by working through the I-you relationship in play, when the experience is fresh and delightful in early childhood. See what happens when you introduce toys like the knitted rabbits (page 16) or the soft doll (page 20), which embody concepts of family, nurturing and relationships. Primarily social creatures, we need others around us in order fully to be ourselves. The first steps to an awareness of ego, therefore, are crucial for the relationships that we experience later in life. To help a child, the adult has to exercise dependability, a loving interest and a positive attitude to life. It is also important to take seriously Friedrich Schiller's definition of being human. In 'Letters upon the Aesthetic Education of Man', he wrote 'The human being is only fully human when he plays – and he is playing only when he is fully human.' Through play, we all, child or adult, can find the resiliency that lies at the core of our 'I'.

The 'I am I' awareness

Developmental psychologist, Ewald Vervaet, has useful insights into the arrival of 'I am I' awareness. During a child's second year, she might ask if a bird has laid an egg, without arriving at the idea that all birds lay eggs through connecting her observation to previous experiences. In the course of her third year, however, the general concept that all birds lay eggs does appear, showing that the child's contact with her environment has undergone a change.

In the first months of life, the child has what is known as a passive contact with her surroundings. Epitomized by taking in through the mouth, this is a participatory consciousness in which there is no division between the self and the other. From four months, there is an increasingly physical contact, manifested primarily through the hands. Soon after the first birthday comes attentive contact, when a child can scribble with a crayon. At 18 months to two years, mental contact appears – the child sees a tree and knows from a source outside herself that it is called a tree. From a few months after the second up to the third birthday appears representational contact with the child's surroundings – she can speak of recent events and have ideas of the near future. And from three until four and a half years, the child can make a conceptual contact, linking different entities and considering whether the possible connection relates to reality or not. She looks for connections, asks how things fit together and sees herself as an entity with connections, too.

The child herself has worked towards this 'I am I' awareness and, like lightning, the astounding revelation can strike her that we live among other 'I's' too. She has perceived differences: that her siblings and parents are not the same as her. The 'terrible twos' are the child beginning to say 'here I am', even if the message is not verbalized as yet. With this self-awareness, a child can develop her strengths and challenge her weaknesses. How we as parents behave towards the child and others, as well as the enveloping cultural and social factors, all play a part in determining the individuality of that child which, from here on, will be revealed and developed in the social context.

Learning to trust your child

When playing with your child it is important to keep these stages in mind, so that your

expectations are in tune with her inner progress. You must avoid the temptation to push her into an accelerated process. Each step needs its own time to be assimilated fully, so that the next step can be taken on a sound and fruitful basis. The key is to trust your child, just as she trusts you. Being oneself is never straightforward, as all our aspects are interwoven. True balance is a very rare virtue. We all move on, forwards and backwards, through time and space, through feeling and thoughts. The healthier our inner core, the better we can cope with the vicissitudes and joys of life. Your child is in preparation for that adventure and the preparation of her self-discovery needs your sensitive support because the effects last a lifetime.

Knitted rabbits

Knitting is enjoying something of a revival and this project is so simple that it makes a good choice for beginners. This is not an activity that your child will want to imitate for she seems to know instinctively that it is too complicated for her to attempt. However, it involves various aspects that are important for the developing child.

CREATIVE MAGIC

For a start, the rhythm of the needles click-clacking against each other is comforting for your child. Making the square requires effort and finishing the pattern (despite interruptions) takes determination: the presence of a working adult involved in something creative provides your child with a wonderful image to learn from as she grows. It is magical experience for her to see how a rabbit can be created out of a square of knitted material. Furthermore, the use of natural materials – natural wool knitting yarn and soft wool stuffing, for example, rather than nylon or acrylic – allows the toddler to develop a sense for quality materials.

KNITTING A FAMILY

A family of any kind, animal or human, represents a 'wholeness' for your toddler. The baby has a mummy and a daddy, and there is always someone to take care of the others. This ideal is a truth for all children, including those from a single-parent family, for it takes two to create a child. Once you have established a simple family of rabbits, you can use the pattern to help the family grow and grow. It is easily altered to make rabbits of different sizes, in a range of different colours and stitches. A rabbit with the purl knitting on the outside will have a bobbly texture, for example, while those with the plain knitting on the outside will be smooth. You can vary the style and colour of the tails and add straight or floppy ears. Depending on the way you stitch the final form, your rabbit can sit, stand or lie down – it is up to you. Finally, you can make the rabbits firm or soft and cuddly, depending on how you stuff them.

PLAYTIME

Your toddler will love to make little scenes for the rabbit family, and you can join in. Lay a green cloth on the floor and play 'meeting rabbits', taking turns

Hints and tips

- Knit rabbits using different thicknesses of yarn (remember to change the size of your knitting needles to match the yarn).
- Use different colours of yarn.
- Use a variety of knitting stitches – plain, purl or stocking – for different textures.
- Stitch the finished forms differently to create different postures.
- For baby rabbits, knit small squares from thin yarn, using smaller needles.
- Make different tails out of balls of wool or, for bigger rabbits, pompoms.

with your toddler to introduce the rabbits to each other. You can build burrows and caves for the rabbits to hide in and hills for them to hop over, and they can visit other animals such as the felt horses (see page 36) who live in the field next door. You can feed the rabbits pretend carrots and water out of little shell dishes. This floor play provides you with the opportunity to interact peacefully and imaginatively with your toddler, with the potential for simple conversation such as 'Good morning little rabbit, and how are you today?'. Soon you will be able to enjoy watching her repeat this play quietly by herself, slowly extending it to include other toys.

Making a knitted rabbit

If you are not a confident knitter, you can cut the initial knitted square and two ear shapes from an old jumper or cardigan. Make sure all the edges are carefully stitched before and after cutting to size, otherwise it will unravel.

You will need

Natural, undyed
   knitting yarn

Two knitting needles
   (approximately
   3.5 mm/⅛ in)

Sewing needle

Sewing thread

Pins

Carded, unspun
   sheep's wool*

Sharp scissors

* Tease unspun sheep's wool before use, pulling gently to separate dense fibres. A comb-like hand 'carder' speeds up the process.

How to do it

1 Knit a 16 cm (6¼ in) square: 1 row plain, 1 row purl (cast on some 40 stitches depending on the thickness of the wool).

2 Knit two ears, casting on 6 stitches and knitting each plain until approximately 6 cm (2½ in) long, then reduce the following 2 rows each by 2 stitches. Cast off the remaining stitches and sew the loose end of yarn into the ear. Cut neatly.

3 Shape the rabbit. Sew each corner of the knitted square together for 5 cm (2 in) to form the four legs. If the purl stitches are on the inside, the finished rabbit will have a smooth texture. If they are on the outside, the rabbit will have a bobbly feel.

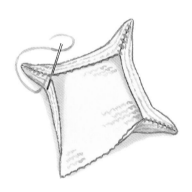

4 Use gathering stitch to sew across the cast-on edge and pull lightly to gather the thread and create the rabbit's head.

5 From this gathered edge, continue sewing a central seam (the rabbit's stomach) to the hind legs. Leave open a space for stuffing.

6 Stuff the rabbit fairly tightly with unspun sheep's wool, especially in the head area. Tie a length of doubled wool around the rabbit's neck, pull tightly and knot to make the head. Tie securely under the chin.

7 Fold the hind legs forward, under the body, and pin. Draw up the open end with gathering stitch and sew in place. Stitch the hind legs to the body, then remove the pins. Shape the body, rounding the hind part.

8 To make an eye, sew a couple of stitches in position to secure the wool, then stitch through to the opposite side of the head and pull gently, indenting the eye area.

9 Sew on the ears, positioning the corners closer together at the sewn edge to make them stand up if desired.

10 Make a tail either by winding knitting yarn around your finger, or by using a tiny pompom or a piece of stuffing wool, and sew in position.

Soft doll

As a young child or toddler becomes more aware of himself, so he becomes more aware of what is taking place around him. He also becomes more objective about what is happening to him. He begins to feel his boundaries – his outer skin. He starts to feel everyday bumps and knocks more deeply, and is able to communicate this to you through speech.

IMITATING LIFE THROUGH PLAY

As he observes the family routine, your toddler starts wanting to 'do' things himself, to act out his observations – to 'play' for the first time. He begins to re-enact situations that he has seen and felt and, using his imagination and fantasy, is able to extend his play and even to play with, or alongside, others.

A doll is a plaything that has a certain reality for your child. He is able to express his own feelings, thoughts, desires and actions through and to the doll – his play becomes a representation of his observations of life itself. It is time for you as parents to stand back and observe your toddler's play, as he rehearses and practises what he has seen, felt and heard.

Hints and tips

- The head should measure approximately one-third of the body length, so adjust accordingly when making dolls of different sizes.
- Change the hair or clothes to make either a boy or girl doll.
- Eyes and mouth could be simply indicated, leaving your child free to imagine the doll's emotions.
- You could use an old vest or t-shirt material for the cotton-knit fabric.

Your child can give this simple doll its own expressions – a good reason for keeping facial features simple. The doll has arms and legs and is firm enough to dress and undress yet still remains cuddly and warm. You can add hair using knitting yarn that is similar in colour to your child's hair. You can match his eye colour, too. This will allow your child to relate even more closely to his doll. For a girl, you could make a doll with longer hair, which can be styled in a number of ways.

A soft doll is absolutely real for your child. She has a name, a character, a whole persona. She hurts, cries, is happy and plays. She enjoys being dressed and undressed, being fed when she is hungry and put to bed when she is tired.

Girls and boys differ in the way that they play, and this becomes more distinct as they grow older. When they are beginning to play imaginatively, they both play house, imitating mother and father. As they reach three or four years old, however, a girl tends to enjoy playing mummy with her baby, while a boy needs a doll that provides him with an opportunity to pour out his feelings to another, who understands and feels, unconditionally, all that he feels. A boy also needs to practise his nurturing skills in the same way that girls do, and he is fortunate if you can positively support his relationship with his doll so that he can begin to relate to the 'other' through his emerging play.

'The favourite doll can become like an alter ego for the child, invested with a bit of the child's own emerging sense of self.'

Rahima Baldwin Dancy, *You are Your Child's First Teacher*

Making a soft doll

You can adjust the measurements given for this project to suit the fabric you have available or to create dolls of different sizes. In each case, be sure to keep the measurements proportional.

You will need

Carded, unspun
  sheep's wool *

Thread or yarn

Dressmaking scissors

White cotton-knit fabric

Sewing needle

Strong sewing thread

Skin-coloured cotton-
  knit fabric

Pins

Embroidery needle

Red and blue or brown
  embroidery thread

Coloured yarn for hair

*Tease unspun sheep's wool
before use, pulling gently to
separate dense fibres. A
comb-like hand 'carder'
speeds up the process.

How to do it

1 Make a firm head for the doll using unspun wool to form a tight ball, about 10 cm (4 in) in height. Wrap the ball in a rough square of unspun wool and tie off the excess with thread or yarn. Leave some excess wool hanging, as it will give stability to the neck.

2 Wrap the head in a square of white cotton-knit fabric and tie with thread or yarn, again leaving any excess hanging.

3 Decide which side of the head is to be the face and smooth any folds (especially around the chin and neck) to the back. Indent the head at eye level by winding strong thread around its circumference and pulling in. Tie a second piece of cotton to the first, roughly where the right ear would be. Pull the thread over the top of the head and tie again to the first thread, roughly where the left ear would be. Now wind the thread down below the head at the back and return to your starting point. Tie well.

4 Neaten the excess wool below the head into a cylinder shape to form the doll's neck, stitching the layers neatly at the back.

5 Wrap the head tightly in skin-coloured fabric, with the grain of the fabric running up and down the face. Overlap the edges at the back of the head, turn under the raw edge and sew a vertical seam. Tie off the neck with strong thread and stitch in place.

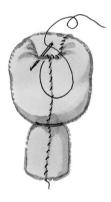

6 Pull the top edge of the skin-coloured fabric to the back of the head, turn under the raw edges and stitch neatly to secure.

7 Mark the eyes and mouth with pins. Using blue or brown embroidery thread for eyes and red for the mouth, sew through the head, from front to side, to make each stitch. Keep the face simple. Remove the pins.

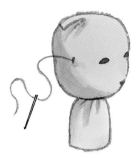

8 Cut a piece of stretchy skin-coloured fabric for the arms, about 30 cm (12 in) × 11 cm (4½ in). Fold in half lengthways, right sides together. Stitch the seams as shown below, leaving a gap in the middle of 8 cm (3¼ in) for the body. Cut a V in the fold for the neck, as shown. Turn right sides out.

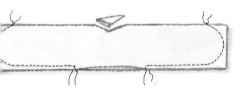

9 Cut another piece of the same fabric for the legs and body, about 22 cm (9 in) wide × 28 cm (11 in) deep. Fold in half widthways, right sides together, and sew a seam down the long edge to create a tube. Stop at the halfway point, where the legs will begin.

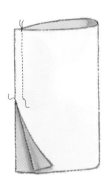

10 Rotate the body/leg fabric, so that the seam is now at the back, and stitch seams for the legs and feet as shown on the illustration. Begin the legs about 14 cm (5½ in) from the bottom edge and start the feet curves about 3 cm (1¼ in) from the bottom edge. Carefully cut between the two legs and around the feet, and turn the fabric right sides out.

Soft doll **23**

11 Stuff the legs, pushing the wool firmly into the feet. Fold each foot up slightly and stitch across the front of the foot, as shown in the illustration, to help the foot stand. Take care not to sew all the way through the foot. Stuff the rest of the leg, leaving a loose 'joint' at the top that will enable the doll to sit. Pin and then stitch across this joint, as shown below, sewing right through from front to back. Remove the pins.

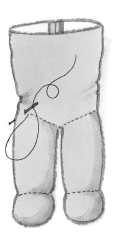

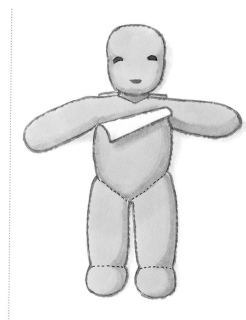

14 Sew the body/leg section in place, stitching together at the shoulders and around the neck and arms to secure.

15 Sew gathering stitches around the wrist and pull tight to form a hand, stitching to secure. Sew on yarn for hair, attaching firmly.

12 To assemble the doll, stuff the arms loosely with unspun wool, leaving the neck/chest area of the arm section empty. Tuck the neck end of the doll's head through the hole in the folded edge of the arm section. Stitch the arm section to the neck leaving about 1 cm (½ in) of neck showing above the shoulders.

13 Make a 2.5 cm (1 in) slit in each side of the body/leg section, from the top where it will meet the arm section. Stuff the body lightly and pull it up over the arm section, up to the shoulders and neck. If necessary, stuff some more, making sure that the arms can hang down comfortably.

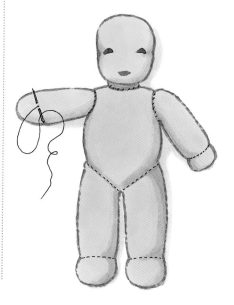

Dolls' clothes

As your child becomes more involved in his imaginative play, he begins to imitate daily life and needs the right toys to be able to do this to his satisfaction. Before this age, he was content simply to rock his doll or feed her with imaginary food. Now he needs implements – a bowl and spoon are required, for example, even if the food is imaginary.

Providing a selection of dolls' clothes for different occasions will stimulate your child's play. He can put a hat and scarf on the doll when he is taking her outside, change her into a summer dress in warm weather or give her a little apron when he is feeding her.

Dressing and undressing is part of everyday life. Your child will enjoy this activity and it provides him with an opportunity to develop precise motor skills. Initially, he will need the dexterity to push a fairly soft doll's arm into a jacket or to pull on some pants. As he grows older, he will want to tie laces or do up buttons on the jacket. He needs to practise all of these small finger movements over and over until the skill is acquired. Eventually, practising dressing a doll will lead your toddler to being able to dress himself. It takes time, practice and patience – the three things your toddler needs to develop into a rounded and capable human being. Leave him to try and try again, and only help when you feel it is really necessary, such as when he becomes upset or frustrated. Show him slowly so that he can try again himself.

These dolls' clothes provide opportunities for your toddler to practise other skills, too. They need to be folded and put away, hung on hangers, washed and dried on the line. Your toddler can iron them with a wooden block on a small table while you are doing the ironing yourself. There is nothing your toddler enjoys more than doing practical domestic activities with you.

Hints and tips
- You can make these clothes to fit any size of doll.
- Choose simple stretchy material, such as old pyjamas, vests and t-shirts.
- Sew on ribbons, buttons and sequins for decoration.

'The serious side of life, with all its demands in daily work, is re-enacted in deep earnestness by the child in its play.'

Rudolf Steiner, *The Child's Changing Consciousness and Waldorf Education*

Making dolls' clothes

These easy-to-make clothes fit the doll measurements suggested on pages 22–24, but can be altered to fit any size of doll.

How to do it

You will need

Dressmaking scissors

Sewing needle

Sewing thread

Embroidery needle

Embroidery thread

Pinking shears (optional)

For a girl doll's clothes

Dress fabric

Stretchy pant fabric

Thin elastic

For a boy doll's clothes

Double-knit yarn in
   two colours

Knitting needles
   (3.5 mm/⅛ in)

Darning needle

Felt

Pencil

Button

Old vest

1 Cut the girl doll's dress fabric. It should fit from shoulder to knee (about 18 cm/7 in), and be about 4 cm (1½ in) wider than the width of the doll front and back (about 33 cm/13 in in total).

2 Fold the dress fabric, right sides together, so the short edges meet in the middle. Cut a slit one-third of the way down from the top of each folded edge for the armholes.

3 Stitch the short edges together and rotate the fabric so the seam is at the back. Sew the front and back of the dress together across the shoulders. Turn right sides out.

4 Use running stitch to gather the neck of the dress with embroidery thread, starting at the back seam. Leave the two ends long enough to tie in a bow. Hem the raw edges or, if the material does not need hemming, cut a pretty edge with pinking shears.

5 Cut a 22 × 10 cm (9 × 4 in) rectangle from the pants fabric and fold, right sides together, so that the short sides meet in the middle. This will be the back seam. Stitch, stopping 1.5 cm (¾ in) short of the top. Cut out a V shape for between the legs.

6 Hem leg edges or cut with pinking shears. Fold the top edge over by 1.5 cm (¾ in) and stitch. Thread the elastic through the hole at the back seam and sew ends together. Stitch the hole closed and turn right sides out.

7 Knit the boy doll's hat. Loosely cast on some 40 stitches (or measure around the doll's head and cast on stitches to the same length). Row 1: knit 1 plain, 1 purl; Row 2: knit 1 purl, 1 plain. Continue with alternate rows for 6 rows. Knit the next 16 rows plain, reducing the length by 1 stitch at the beginning of each row (24 stitches remaining). Cast off.

8 Gather the top of the hat and stitch the back seam using the darning needle.

9 Make a pompom from a different colour. Wind a length of yarn 25 times around your finger. Thread a short length of yarn through the centre of the wound loops and tie a tight knot. Stitch to the hat and cut through the loops to create a pompom. Trim the ends to finish.

10 To make the scarf, cast on 10 stitches. Row 1: 1 plain, 1 purl; Row 2: 1 purl, 1 plain. Continue with alternate rows until the scarf measures 40 cm (16 in). Cast off. Add the tassels by looping through yarn of a different colour and tying with a knot.

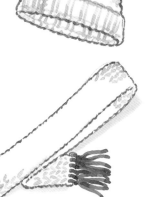

Blanket stitch

Take the needle from the front to the back of the fabric, 2–3 mm (⅛ in) from the edge. Repeat the first stitch again, using the same entrance hole. Working from left to right, make a second stitch about 2–3 mm (⅛ in) from the first. Ensure the loop comes behind the needle. Pull the thread so that the loop lies on the top of the material, and continue. When you come to the end, complete by making another double stitch.

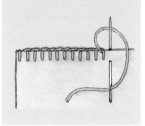

11 To make the shorts/trousers, cast on 42 stitches (or measure around the doll's waist and cast on stitches to the same length). Row 1: knit 1, plain 1, purl; Row 2: knit 1, purl 1, plain and continue for 4 rows. Knit plain until shorts/trousers measure from the waist to the top of the legs (about 18 rows).

12 Now knit half the stitches (21) and slip the remaining stitches onto a spare needle. Continue to knit one leg until it reaches the required length for shorts or trousers, keeping count of the rows knitted, and knitting the last two rows in a different colour. Cast off. Re-join the wool to the second leg and knit to match. Cast off.

13 Using the darning needle and matching yarn, stitch up the shorts/trousers from the waist to the crotch. Then stitch the leg seams. Sew a length of contrasting yarn around the waist and tie in a bow.

14 To make the boy's jacket, fold the felt in half and draw a simple design with the shoulders running along the folded edge (see illustration to Step 15). It should be about 20 cm (8 in) across by 12 cm (5 in) down. Cut a shallow area in the centre of the folded edge for the neck, open out the felt and cut a seam running up the centre of the jacket front.

15 Fit the jacket, marking the position of the side seams. Trim the excess fabric away from the side seams, then oversew the seams together (see page 39) using thread the same colour as the jacket fabric.

16 Use embroidery thread of a contrasting colour to sew around neck, arm, front and bottom edges in blanket stitch (see box). Stitch a buttonhole and attach a button using the same thread.

17 To make a vest, measure the doll's body and cut a piece of fabric from an old vest (with the grain running vertically up and down) that measures slightly more than the width of the body and twice the length. Fold in half, right sides together, and sew the side seams, leaving openings for the arms. Cut out a scoop in the centre of the folded edge for the neck. Hem the raw edges and turn right sides out.

Doll's swing seat

Swinging is a rhythmical activity enjoyed by all, but particularly by the young child. We all know how soothing rhythmic movements are, whether in stroking and rocking a baby or bouncing and swinging a toddler. The child relaxes into the timeless movement, asking for 'more' each time the bouncing comes to an end.

A HEALING ACTIVITY

Swinging is actually healing for a young child, particularly if you accompany it with singing. Your toddler will love being pushed in a swing at the park, while you sing the simple age-old nonsense rhyme below over and over again, to the tune of 'See-saw Marjory Daw'. To begin with, you can stand in front of the swing and push your child so that she feels no fear, before moving to stand behind her.

Sing, sing, swing, swing
The cat's gone off with the pudding bag string.
Do, do, what shall I do?
The cat has bitten it quite in two.

Hints and tips
- Use strong material.
- These instructions will fit a toy about 30 cm (12 in) long, but can be adapted to fit any size of toy.
- Garden cane makes good dowelling.
- Use string or knitting yarn for the hanging cords or twist your own from strong embroidery thread or thin wool.
- Hang the swing from a branch or a broom handle propped across pieces of furniture.

LEARNING FROM EXPERIENCE

With this doll's swing, your child can express her love of swinging in another way – that is, by imitating you and becoming the parent pushing her favourite toy. The swing is really easy to make and can be suspended from a small branch in the garden, or from a broom handle balanced across two chairs when indoors. The doll fits comfortably on the seat, with her arms tucked behind the side strings so that she does not fall. Sing with your toddler as she pushes her doll backwards and forwards, standing in front of or behind the swing. She will soon come to understand the rules of balance and motion from this activity alone – if she goes too high, the doll will fall out!

Should this happen, however, you should react in the same way that you would if your own child had fallen, picking the doll up and comforting her with a little cuddle, before putting her back in the swing. This way, your toddler will learn to respect and care for the doll. She will also learn that you need to attach the swing firmly to the branch or stick, in order to stop it slipping and overbalancing the doll. These are lessons for life, and learning them now from experience (you don't need to explain to her in words) is the best way for her to relate them also to herself.

Making a doll's swing seat

You can easily adapt the design for this swing seat for any toy, large or small. Simply adjust the measurements to fit.

How to do it

You will need

Fabric

Dressmaking scissors

Pins

Sewing needle

Sewing thread

5 mm (¼ in)
  cane dowelling

Saw

Sandpaper

Craft knife

Hanging cord

PVA glue

1 Cut a 28 × 16 cm (11 × 6¼ in) piece of fabric and hem the long sides.

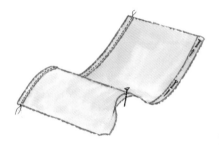

2 Cut three lengths of dowelling, each 3 cm (1¼ in) longer than the short edge of the fabric, and sand the ends smooth. With the fabric lying flat, wrong side up, lay a dowel at each short end, fold the end of the fabric tightly over each and stitch firmly in place.

3 Repeat with the third length of dowelling, stitching it approximately 12 cm (5 in) in from one end. This shorter section forms the seat of the swing.

4 Use a craft knife to score a notch at each end of the top and bottom lengths of dowelling for the hanging cord. Cut two lengths of cord, each about three to four times as long as the swing seat. Tie one end of a cord around a notched end of the top dowel and glue in place.

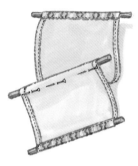

5 Tie the other end of the cord around the notched end of the bottom dowel and glue in place. Repeat with the other cord.

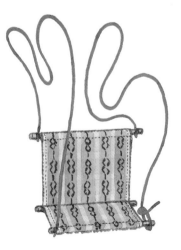

Doll's sling

Your toddler can remember how it felt to be carried, rocked and held by you when she was little. The experience lives within her and the desire for this comforting gesture is still there. Many parents today follow the work of Jean Liedloff, who, in her book *The Continuum Concept*, advocates an 'in-arms phase', which should extend between birth and crawling.

This is practised in many countries of the developing world, where mothers carry their babies on their backs or in a sling across their front. The rhythm of their movement, as they walk or work in the fields or do housework, soothes the baby. In Western culture however, people busy themselves with many different activities at the same time – answering the phone, doing the laundry and cooking. These hurried movements are not always rhythmical and can be disturbing for the baby.

ON THE MOVE

Now that your toddler is more active, she wants to be on the move, as does her doll or favourite bear. In fact, leaving the doll or bear behind could be as difficult for your toddler as it would be for you to leave your child. Carrying the doll in a little sling is one way in which your toddler can happily take her toy for a walk, to the park, shopping or wherever you happen to be going.

A SENSE OF INDEPENDENCE

Encouraging your toddler to wear the sling is also a way in which you can help her to become more independent when you are out together. It is not something that she can use while sitting in a buggy, so she will have to be walking beside you if she wants to carry it. Although it may take longer to get anywhere, walking will have very positive effects on your child, strengthening her limbs and allowing her to breathe more deeply and walk rhythmically. All these things help her to develop a strong physical body and a healthy tiredness that results in a good night's sleep.

The sling can be worn on the front or on the back. Many girls prefer to wear it on the front, in imitation of the mothers they see around them, carrying their babies close to their hearts in a timeless gesture of protection. Boys may prefer carrying a doll on the back, leaving their arms free to work and play unencumbered. Whichever way they wear the sling to carry their doll, be ready for it to come off when they get tired of the novelty – and into your bag!

Hints and tips

- Your toddler can wear the sling over the shoulders as a rucksack or on the front like a baby carrier.
- Your toddler can open the sling flat to use it as a 'changing' mat for her doll.
- This sling fits a 35–45 cm (14–18 in) doll, but can be adapted to work for any favourite toy.

Making a doll's sling

By encouraging your toddler to use this sling, you can make her feel 'responsible' for her doll. It also means that the doll is not easily left behind, lost or dropped anywhere.

How to do it

You will need

Strong fabric

Dressmaking scissors

Sewing needle

Sewing thread

Thin padding

Pins

4 large poppers/ press studs

Tailor's chalk

1 Cut a 90 x 20 cm (36 x 8 in) length of material and fold in half, wrong sides out, to bring the two short edges together.

2 Now fold the bottom (folded) edge up so that the lower half measures 18 cm (7 in). Cut the corners where the doll's legs will go. They should reach approximately 4 cm (1½ in) up from the second fold.

3 Open out the second fold and sew the long edges of fabric together from bottom to top, leaving the top open for the padding.

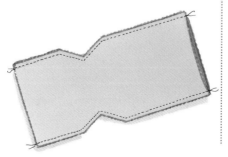

4 Cut a piece of padding to fit inside the back section of the sling without bunching. Turn the fabric right sides out and insert the padding.

5 Cut two straps from the remaining fabric, each measuring 65 x 8 cm (25 x 3¼ in). Fold each down the length, right sides together, and stitch the raw edges. Turn right sides out and press flat. Tack one end of each strap to the inside face of the sling, one in each corner, then fold down a small hem along both raw edges of the opening and tack or pin in place. Then pin the two sides together and stitch to close the opening and secure the straps. Remove tacking stitches and pins.

6 Turn the sling over and sew press studs/poppers on the outside face of the sling, one in each corner just above the fold. Sew corresponding press studs/poppers 1.5 cm (¾ in) from the end of each strap. To wear the sling, attach the straps to the press studs/poppers.

7 On the inside face of the sling, fold the lower section into position and use tailor's chalk to mark the locations of two more pairs of press studs/poppers that will secure the front of the sling to the back once the doll is in position. Stitch them firmly in place.

Felt horse

Sewing is a great domestic activity, providing a positive image of a working adult for your toddler to imitate. Unlike knitting, young children feel drawn to imitate sewing. You could give your toddler a little sewing basket containing some felt and a large needle and thread. This will enable him to begin to be creative and start to sew for himself once you have shown him the technique.

EARLY CREATIVITY

The needle should have a point that your toddler can push through the fabric – you do not want him to be frustrated with inadequate tools. If you show him how to use a needle correctly, he will rarely prick himself. Teach him to put the sewing away properly when he has finished, too.

It does not matter what he makes or whether it is anything recognizable. Young children lack a conscious idea of how a toy should look and anything they create looks right to them if you treat it with respect. Imitating real work delights your toddler and just being able to sit and work by you will satisfy him. As he grows, he will become more skilful and more creative, which will lead to him wanting to make more recognizable toys. There are many simple patterns available that your child will be able to attempt when he reaches five or six years old, such as a simple bag, pincushion or felt book with 'pictures'.

DRAWING ON NATURE

The horse is an animal that appeals to all children. They love to see horses running free in the fields and to watch riders clip-clopping down the road. The sounds, movement and beauty of this strong animal appeal to all children, and to make a horse for your toddler's play will add a new friend to the farmyard. At around the same time that you make the horse, take your toddler to see the real thing, not only in the field but at work as well. What a gift the image of a working horse will be, whether you show him a police horse, a racehorse or a horse working on the farm.

Think about colour carefully. Your horse could be grey, black or chestnut colour with the mane and tail the same or in contrast. You could also use a

---

Hints and tips

- Use thick felt and strong cotton to oversew the seams (see page 39).
- If machine-stitching, make the legs thicker to allow for seams.
- If the legs splay out, make a few stitches at the top of the front and back leg seams.
- Make sure you stuff the horse firmly.
- For a neater finish, make the length of the hoof oval slightly smaller than the length of the foot.
- Use a contrasting colour for the eyes, inner ears, head gusset and hooves.

third colour for the hooves and the flash on the forehead. Do keep the colours realistic, however. There are no pink horses in real life.

PLAYTIME

Children love to be bounced up and down to the rhythm of a nursery rhyme and there are many songs to choose from that will introduce different images of a horse to your toddler. The traditional nursery rhyme 'Ride a cock horse to Banbury Cross' is a popular choice. Another favourite is this more modern rhyme, which should be sung with a clip-clop rhythm while bouncing:

Horsie, Horsie don't you stop,
Just let your hooves go clippity clop,
Your tail goes swish and the wheels go round,
Giddy up we're homeward bound.

Making a felt horse

You can use this basic pattern to make a family of horses in a range of different sizes. To make a riding horse, add a felt saddle and bridle.

You will need

Tracing paper

Pencil

Pins

30 x 30 cm (12 x 12 in) thick felt

Scraps of coloured felt

Sharp scissors

Embroidery needle

Embroidery thread

Carded, unspun sheep's wool*

PVA glue

Knitting yarn

*Tease unspun sheep's wool before use, pulling gently to separate dense fibres. A comb-like hand 'carder' speeds up the process.

How to do it

1 Make a paper template by using a photocopier to enlarge the illustration below to the desired size or by drawing a pattern yourself, following the proportions of the illustration. The recommended minimum measurements for your horse are 16 cm (6½ in) nose to tail and 10 cm (4 in) head to hoof. A and B mark the position of the head gusset. You will need two bodies, two inside leg pieces, one head gusset, four hooves, two outside ears, two contrasting inside ears and two eyes. Pin the pattern pieces to the felt and cut out.

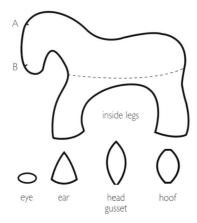

eye   ear   head gusset   hoof

2 Use backstitch to sew the inside leg pieces together along the centre seam and turn the seam to the inside.

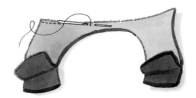

3 Now oversew (see box) the outside leg edges of the body sections to the inside leg piece.

4 Oversew the hooves in place and stuff the legs firmly.

5 Stitch up the back of the horse, leaving a gap at the lower back for stuffing, until you reach point A, where the head gusset will be inserted, as marked on the pattern. Then stitch up the chest and neck and down the chin until you reach point B, where the head gusset will end. Oversew the head gusset in place. Stuff the head and neck firmly.

6 Stuff the horse and complete the sewing.

7 Glue the inner ear to the outer ear and sew firmly to the head on either side. Glue on the eyes and stitch to secure. Embroider circular pupils in the eyes, if liked.

8 To make the tail, wind a length of knitting yarn loosely around four fingers eight to 12 times. Sew through this loop to the rear end of the horse. Wind a length of yarn around the sewn-on area, and cut through the loop at the end of the tail. Trim to neaten.

9 Repeat the process with the mane, sewing on several smaller, individual loops of yarn. Trim to neaten.

Oversewing

This is a useful stitch for joining the edges of felt pieces. Working from left to right, bring the needle through from the back to the front (right to left) of the fabric at a 45-degree angle. Repeat, keeping the stitches small and even.

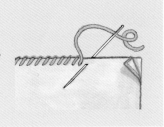

Imagination

Imagination

We both appreciate and denigrate imagination. It is the source of all creativity, technology and culture and yet, because it seems to have no practical or physical reality, we rarely acknowledge imagination for what it is. It is often associated with childhood, as something to be 'grown out of'. It is through our imagination, however, that we find and relate to our world and the imaginative play of childhood starts us on this course.

The playground of the mind

According to Johan Huizinga in his remarkable book on play in human culture, *Homo Ludens,* 'The play-ground of the mind is a world of its own… There things have a different physiognomy from the one they wear in ordinary life, and are bound by ties other than those of logic and causality.' Imagination is the way in which we create images that are not present to our senses. We use this ability once our senses are developed enough to be able to deal with the world. It is also closely connected to our values and moral purpose, since studies have found unimaginative children more likely than imaginative children to turn to violence: when faced with a threatening or humiliating situation they are unable to imagine any response other than aggression. This is especially the case in a culture that bombards children with images showing violence as the only solution to an emotionally demanding situation.

Our imagination is where we piece together our fractured world and, for children, it is a counterpart to expanding awareness. A baby is at one with the world, in the first phase of physical development. At that time, the life forces are engaged in learning to control the limbs and to speak. By the time the child is a toddler, the life forces 'spill over', in Steiner's words, into the mind and imagination. A child will use his imagination to transform everyday things so that they lose their original purpose. A table can become a car, a chair a castle, a cloth the sky, and so on. The child breathes creativity into the world of objects and the inanimate world becomes one of life. According to Bruno Bettelheim in *The Uses of Enchantment,* 'the child's thinking remains animistic until the age of puberty. His parents and teachers tell him that things cannot feel and act; as much as he may pretend to believe this to please adults, or not to be ridiculed, deep down the child knows better.' In his imagination the child finds a relationship to everything around him.

The power of imagination

The words 'creative', 'wellbeing' and 'happiness' represent today's lifestyle ideals. Look at any two- to three-year-old child and you will see how he expresses these ideals without even trying. Perhaps we can learn something from his imaginative faculties. Steiner frequently exhorts teachers to

practise their imagination, and this, in fact, is a prerequisite for teaching in a Steiner school. For example, all lessons should feature imaginative pictures that children can relate to and learn from, rather than purely informative abstractions, because such images are an integral part of the self-education that relates the inner world to the outer one.

During the early years it is the imagination of the child, not the adult, that is paramount: the teacher, or carer, is merely a facilitator. In his lecture cycle, *The Kingdom of Childhood*, Steiner stated: 'The intelligence never penetrates as deeply into reality as fantasy does. Fantasy can go astray, it is true, but it is rooted in reality, whereas the intellect remains

In our increasingly technological world, the images we think in need to be rehearsed in a positive manner as never before. The Romantic poets and artists realized this at the beginning of the Industrial Revolution, but they were often lone voices considered to be in opposition to the practicalities of daily life. In his poem 'The World is Too Much with Us', Wordsworth warned that, unless we could attend to the creative power of imagination, 'In getting and spending, we lay waste our powers.'

Today, we take the Romantic view seriously and are reassessing the importance of the imaginative faculties of childhood for individual development. For the children of today it is imperative that such powers are enhanced and exercised whenever possible. Our way of life and scientific skills can easily remove us from the realities of life into a virtual reality created by others. Through imaginative play, a child can learn to form loving relationships based on respect and empathetic understanding, allowing him to find new and positive ways to confront the problems of the modern world.

always on the surface.' This may seem a somewhat extravagant claim but if you observe the complete immersion of a toddler in his play, you can perceive that he is living in what, for him, is reality. This observation can lead us to consider what our reality really is. How far does it lie within our internal images accessed through our personal imaginative capacities? Imagination knows no time in a worldly sense. For children, simple games, uncomplicated toys, unpressurized time, attentiveness and a subduing of inhibitions can open up this realm.

'Unless you become like little children you will never enter the kingdom of heaven.' Many religions contain a similar thought. This is not a call to a second childishness, but to an awakening of the imaginative sensibilities, so that we can participate in the world in a fruitful way. The child becomes our teacher. But unlike the child in his play, there are consequences when we go astray and so imagination must also have a moral aspect that we learn as we grow. In giving pictures and narratives to our children, we should ensure that, through our mutual imaginative play or storytelling, we bring in values that are nourishing and good.

Harnessing imaginative thought

Great scientists and artists acknowledge that imagination lies at the root of discovery. Einstein, for example, recommended the telling of fairy tales to nurture wisdom in a child. In fact, one could claim that all professions and crafts need an element of imagination for success, that we create a picture of our goals before we attain them. That picture can, and does, adjust as we go along, but it is imagination that allows us the freedom to change. Schools are now expected to give time to social and emotional learning in their curriculum. This is a welcome change, as long as we acknowledge that such skills lie in the imagination and cannot derive from simply dressing up old precepts in new guises.

As economic pressures on individuals and communities increase, creativity is now seen as the key to future prosperity. A 2004 report by thinktank Demos called *Europe in the Creative Age* stresses the importance of the three Ts – talent, technology and tolerance – to stand beside the three Rs in order for any country to prosper. Although intended as a recommendation for the adult world of commerce, these concepts are exactly what a child practises through his natural imaginative play. Our talents are closely bound to our selves. Every child has talents or gifts that can be developed throughout life, but never more so than in our earliest years. They may vary from alertness of mind to kindness of heart, and at this age, as the self emerges, they are revealed in play. This is where, as a parent, you can help your toddler foster his inborn gifts and overcome his weaknesses. Accepting every child as talented engenders self-confidence and the courage to overcome obstacles. These qualities are fragile, however, and a child putting himself imaginatively in new situations needs your uncritical support.

Reality and imagination

Play is a time when we manipulate the world to our liking. When a child moves the furniture in the dolls' house (see pages 54 and 58), piles up blocks and planks (see page 51) or dresses up (see page 66), he is using his hands to change the world in a way devised by his imagination. Imagination tells us that another prospect is possible; we have an intention and in pursuing it we enhance our skills.

At this age, children in play are naturally tolerant if their surroundings allow it. They teach each other how to play, change their games to fit the personalities involved, welcome all participants and cannot abide watching without participating. Play can embrace all and is an exercise in empathetic imagination, in putting oneself in the shoes of another. Playing together is tolerance in practice. When you play creatively with your child he is interested in what you do, too. Playing together is fascinating, because all players can contribute

something and in this way we can learn to accept change without it appearing threatening or foreign.

So, reality and imagination are not two worlds but one, and a child at this age is quite at home with either, with no need to consciously transpose himself. He is there, and that is that. His reality is synonymous with his imagination. As adults we may feel there is great dichotomy between reality and imagination, but that underestimates how the images we form in our minds dictate our reality. To balance our lives, we should listen to our poets and children, for whom, as Huizinga pointed out, imagination and fantasy 'lie beyond seriousness' where we can 'forsake man's wisdom for a child's'. Our language, culture, behaviour, experiences, judgements on right or wrong and loving (or otherwise) relationships are part and parcel of a world of images. There are many books on child development, but very few actually mention the word 'imagination'. Perhaps we have to accept that our children know about this better than we do and that, when it comes to understanding this part of our lives, poetic understanding comes closer to the truth than analytical observation.

Riding horse

As your toddler becomes more active and better able to control her movement and balance, she will seek out toys that require an element of physical skill so that she can play in a different way. The impulse to move is very strong, and children love nothing more than to run, jump, hop, skip and gallop – all movements that require repetition and rhythm.

THE UNFOLDING IMAGINATION

Her ability to ride a horse like this one will take time and practice, and playing with it will help to develop her physical body and muscles without any conscious effort. However, it is not only the physical that is developing here but also the imagination. This toy helps the imagination develop in many different ways.

In one kindergarten, a five-year-old boy and two four-year-old girls each had a riding horse. They dressed up as a prince and princesses and rode out into the 'wide, wide world' having adventures. On the way, they stopped to feed their horses and this became a central activity of the play, drawing in other children who provided the shop from which they bought the food (conkers from the chestnut tree) that they fed to the horses in little baskets before continuing on their travels. This play continued for weeks on end, transforming day by day. The children cared for the horses appropriately, feeding them, watering them and putting them to bed, and developed a healthy respect for them. Their galloping and trotting (or walking when the game became too noisy!) helped develop their sense of rhythm and, of course, aided the development of a strong physical body.

This is a very simple example of how a child's imagination can unfold on a day-to-day basis. In this toy riding horse your toddler will find a true companion, naming it with fondness. She will care for the horse, tying it up securely at night or when it is not in play. You can add to it by sewing bells onto the reins or making colourful headbands. You will find it brings joy to your child's play and helps her fantasy life to develop.

Your child's developing imagination needs feeding with a certain reality before it can find expression in play. As your child grows, it is a good idea to visit a farm or stable, where she can observe horses in real life, feed them and watch them move in a field. This will make an enormous difference to her play, which will develop a new dimension and become even more creative.

Hints and tips

- Use a natural, light-coloured sock (brown or grey).
- Sand and varnish the pole before inserting it into the sock.
- You could place a piece of material over the top of the pole before inserting it to provide extra padding and to protect the sock.
- For reins, use thick string, braid or ribbon.
- For a rolling horse, drill a hole through the bottom of the pole and add wheels on a dowel.

Making a riding horse

You will need

1 small adult cotton or wool sock

Carded, unspun sheep's wool*

85–100 cm (33–40 in) pole, 1.5–3 cm (¾– 1¼ in) in diameter

Sandpaper

Screwdriver and short flathead screw

Sewing needle and thread

Elastic band (optional)

Tracing paper and pencil

Pins

Felt or leather offcuts

Thin fabric padding

Dressmaking scissors

Embroidery needle and embroidery thread

Thick knitting yarn

2 metre (2 yard) length braid or ribbon

2 curtain rings

4 bells

80 cm (32 in) thick cord

PVA glue

You can use a broomstick to make the pole for this riding horse, but make sure you trim it down to a comfortable height for your child before using.

How to do it

1 Pack the sock tightly up to the heel with unspun sheep's wool. Sand both ends of the pole. Insert one end into the stuffed sock, ensuring the top of the pole is well padded.

2 Finish stuffing the back of the head and neck area tightly and tie the neck of the sock around the pole. Screw through the padding and into the top of the pole to stop it slipping about. Bend the sock at the neck area (the heel) and stitch where the head and neck meet to bend the sock into shape.

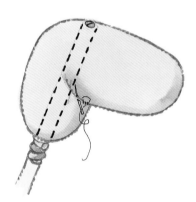

*Tease unspun sheep's wool before use, pulling gently to separate dense fibres. A comb-like hand 'carder' speeds up the process.

3 Tie a thread or elastic band around the nose area (the sock toe) to give it shape. Pull in at the mouth and stitch to secure.

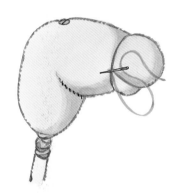

4 Draw an ear outline on tracing paper, pin to the darker leather or felt offcuts and cut out two. Then pin to the lighter-coloured offcuts and cut out two more. Cut two more shapes from the thin fabric padding.

5 Layer each ear, with the darker colour first, then the padding, then the lighter piece, and stitch together using blanket stitch (see page 28) and embroidery thread.

6 Bring the two bottom corners of each ear together and stitch to hold in place.

7 To make the horse's mane, wind a length of knitting yarn loosely around three fingers a few times to make a bundle of loops. You will need several of these. Sew each bundle tightly and securely to the head, starting at the front between the future ear positions and working backwards down the neck towards the pole. Cut the loops and fluff up.

8 Pin the ears in position and sew them securely to the head before trimming the mane to neaten.

10 To make the harness, cut a length of braid to fit across the nose from one side of the mouth to the other, and a second length to fit under the chin. Sew each section onto a curtain ring.

11 Measure a third and fourth length of braid to run from each of the rings to the mane. Sew in place under the mane or behind the ears. Sew a fifth piece of braid under the chin. If desired, attach a piece of cord across the brow at the front of the ears, linking the two strips of braid. Attach bells to the rings on both sides.

9 Draw an eye outline on tracing paper, pin to felt offcuts and cut out two felt eyes. Cut out two felt circles in a contrasting colour for the pupils. Pin in position on the horse and stitch in place.

12 Attach cord for the reins to the rings and tie well. Finally, cut a length of felt or fabric and glue over the join where the sock meets the pole. Sew the seam to secure.

Building blocks and planks

Now that your toddler is becoming more skilful with his movements and in his balance, he will enjoy creating different things with the blocks and planks you provide. In the first two years, it took all his skill simply to build a tower, which he took as much delight in knocking down as he did in building up (often with your help). Now his play will change.

As your toddler's play becomes more creative and imaginative, he will use the blocks and planks in different ways. A range of shapes and sizes will allow him to practise balancing and inspire him to become more adventurous with his buildings.

Show your toddler how easy it is to make a bridge by balancing a small plank or length of bark across two logs. More logs can be used to make a fence or a house with a bark roof. Together you can make a shed for the felt horse (see page 36) or a hutch for the rabbit family (see page 16). As your toddler becomes more skilful, he can use larger blocks as stepping stones across a pond filled with fish (see page 62). Make a bridge with a long plank balanced on two logs and he will delight in crossing over it. You can also prop a long plank on a cushion and use it as a hillside for a wooden car or train to come down or as a slide for a doll. Make a see-saw by balancing the plank over a circular log and the two of you can enjoy rocking dolls up and down, singing some rocking nursery rhymes.

A SHARED ACTIVITY

Look for small branches and different shaped logs while out on walks with your toddler. Peeling bark from fallen trees is a wonderful activity, particularly when your toddler discovers the little creatures hidden underneath. Pine cones make trees for a forest, while acorns, horse chestnuts or other seeds will feed the animals, feeding your child's imagination at the same time. All these natural materials help your toddler develop an appreciation for the abundance around him, especially if you treat each find with the wonder it deserves.

Preparing the various found objects with your toddler provides him with an opportunity for sorting, cleaning and preparing his playthings with care. Once play has finished, your toddler can sort the toys into different-sized baskets, ready for play the next day.

Hints and tips
- Wood should be well seasoned before use to avoid cracking or splintering. Dry pieces in a kiln or air-dry outside then keep indoors for a week or two.
- Check any bark is firmly in place. If not, peel it off.
- Choose pieces of wood without cracks or splinters.
- Planks should be sturdy enough for children to stand on.

Making blocks and planks

When you have found some suitable logs, branches, sticks and bark pieces, prepare them for play by sawing off any rough edges. You must also season them before use, letting them dry out in the fresh air to prevent them going mouldy (see page 51).

How to do it

You will need

Offcuts of wood

Seasoned logs, branches and sticks of different types and sizes

Seasoned bark

Saw

Electric sander

Sandpaper

Boiled linseed oil or olive oil and cloths

1 For smooth wooden blocks and planks, choose nice pieces of wood and saw to different lengths.

2 For rough wood and bark blocks, choose firm pieces that are well seasoned and saw to different lengths. Cut some in half lengthways as well.

3 If necessary, round the corners of the blocks and planks with an electric sander. Use sandpaper to sand all the sawn surfaces smoothly.

4 Oil all the blocks and planks with boiled linseed oil and rub with a cloth once the oil has soaked in.

Dolls' house

A dolls' house provides an opportunity for your young child to play with his own representation of a home. You will find this stimulates a different sort of imaginative play as he begins to imitate what is happening in his own home, playing out different situations with the dolls. Dolls' houses are often more suitable for an older child.

INTRODUCING NEW IDEAS

A three-year-old might need some interaction on your part to help the process begin, while a four-year-old will play with the house endlessly. Placing the house at the centre of a scene provides a greater opportunity for your toddler's imagination to develop. For example, if it is a house for a family, it will need a table and chairs, a bedroom and so on, all of which can be inside the house. But you can become more adventurous and make houses of different types and sizes, with rooms added onto the original building – a bedroom or a kitchen, for instance. Another building can be a barn for the horses. Balance the house on some blocks to provide another level and the animals can shelter underneath or your toddler can use the space for parking his cars. Build steps up to the house by placing different-sized logs in a row. All these variations provide a wonderful opportunity for you to interact with your toddler and to develop new ideas together.

He will also enjoy playing with his friends, using just the house at first but eventually building and extending it endlessly, as he begins to get more and more ideas, to include outside spaces such as a farmyard or even a neighbouring house. The toys who live in the houses will visit each other and can travel around, feeding the animals and rounding up the horses. This sort of play encourages social interaction, particularly for the younger toddler who tends to play alongside rather than with other children. He learns to integrate when his attention is focused outside himself.

EXERCISING THE IMAGINATION

Using simple toys and props for the house, either made ones (see page 58) or things that you have collected from natural sources, provides scope for your child's imagination to develop. Include some unfinished forms so that your toddler can let his imagination decide what the object is. A perfectly moulded and coloured plastic strawberry can only ever be a strawberry, while a pretty shell can become a dish, a piece of food, a mouse or a hat, depending on its shape and size. It can be anything your child wants it to be.

Hints and tips
- Cut the base to size or shape from a plank of wood or a corner shelf.
- Make houses of different sizes depending on the bases you have to hand.
- A slightly rougher base makes a good start for a stable for the animals or a garage for cars.
- Have a number of differently coloured cloths for the covering.

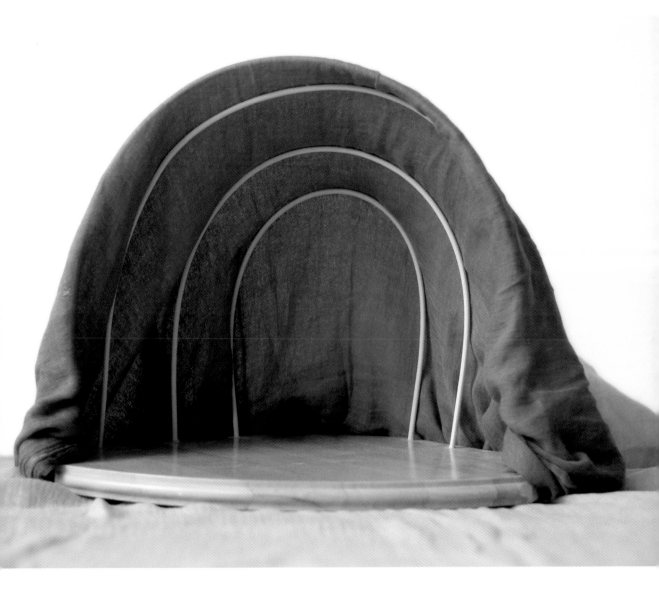

'What a difference there is between… playthings that leave as much as possible to the power of imagination and giving finished toys that leave nothing for the child's own inner activity.'

Rudolf Steiner, *The Roots of Education*

Making a dolls' house

This simple dolls' house can be adapted as a farm, a home, a stable or a cave. By changing the colour of the cloth, you can transform the house to suit different aspects of play.

How to do it

1 Use a pencil to draw the outline of the base on the wood. Place the wood in a vice and cut out the shape using a saw or jigsaw.

2 Round and sand all edges well.

3 Mark the wooden base with holes for the cane. The cane needs to reach from one side of the base to the other, so make sure the holes are parallel and roughly 5 cm (2 in) apart. Drill the holes using a drill bit that is the same diameter as the cane.

4 Use cane cutters to cut lengths of cane to size, increasing the length slightly for each one. This will give you a nicely shaped roof. For a 35 cm (14 in) wide base, the height could be 25 cm (10 in) at the front, tapering to 18 cm (7 in) at the back.

5 Glue the ends of the cane into the drilled holes. Polish the base and cane with boiled linseed oil, rubbing with a cloth once the oil has soaked in.

6 Cut the thin fabric so that it can drape easily over the house, covering it completely from the roof at the front to the floor at the back, and covering both sides. Hem the fabric before draping it over the house.

Dolls' house furniture

Your toddler loves to imitate what she sees in the world around her. The dolls' house (see page 54), which may become a representation of her own home, would simply not be complete without furniture. It is important to provide opportunity for your child to discover new things for herself. The right toys help children to re-enact experiences from life.

When a young child discovers her world, everything is new to her. She looks at things with different eyes to those of an adult. When we see something, we react with our thoughts before reacting with our actions. When a child sees something happening around her, she reacts with her will – immediately. Play occupies a position for her that, for adults, is occupied by our experiences, ideas and thoughts. A child needs to be able to play out her experiences in order for them to become her own, for her to form a relationship with them. Therefore, she needs to be active in her play, imitating her surroundings.

REFLECTING WHAT SHE SEES

Providing furniture for her house must be done with careful thought. Firstly, the furniture should relate to the home she lives in. Think about what is most important to her at this age – probably somewhere to sleep and somewhere to eat – and begin with pieces for a bedroom and a kitchen/dining area. A small table and chairs, a little bed and perhaps a lamp make a perfect start. These pieces should be simple enough for you to make and finish off with your toddler's help. If your child watches you as you work, you will provide a wonderful role model for her. She can help, by screwing the tabletop into the base for example, and then you can sand and polish everything together. In this way, she develops an appreciation for the will and effort you put into making and completing the toys with such care and love. This will encourage her to treat them with care too.

You can provide details for the house later: a cloth for the table, little shells for plates, a carpet carefully hemmed and fringed, a pillow and cover for the bed and a lampshade to give light. Once you begin, your child will soon add ideas of her own and the whole experience becomes truly creative for you both.

Your toddler's play will become ever more creative as she finds ways to use her imagination, such as making tea for her doll family, putting a baby doll to bed, tending a garden filled with trees (pine cones) or flowers (cut from your garden and put into small vases), or growing vegetables (upturned seedheads) behind the house. Don't

Hints and tips

- Choose branches of the right size to make furniture that fits comfortably in the house.
- Season wood before use (see page 51).
- You can leave the bark on, if smooth and secure.
- Use fabric scraps for rugs, blankets and tablecloths.
- Hem the edges of the cloth for soft furnishings.
- Use shells for plates.

forget to provide cloths of different colours, which can transform the outside area into a garden pond surrounded by logs or shells, or a meadow in which the horses graze, or a garden plot filled with plants.

The table and chairs can come outside on nice days, when the family can picnic. The ideas are endless and you will find your own imagination stimulated by your toddler's play.

Making dolls' house furniture

You will need

Seasoned branches of
   wood in different sizes

Saw

Drill and drill bits

Screwdriver

Small flathead screw

Wood filler

Scraps of fabric

Chisel

Matchsticks

PVA glue

Thin dowelling

Thin card

Adhesive putty

Sandpaper

Boiled linseed oil or olive
   oil and cloths

Dolly pegs

Scraps of felt

Sewing needle

Sewing thread

Sharp scissors

Knitting yarn

Pencil crayons

You can make any furniture you like but start with a few recognizable staples, such as a bed, a table and chairs – pieces that will be familiar to your toddler from her own home.

How to do it

1 To make a table, choose a smooth log or branch for the stand and cut to the required height. Cut the table top from a wider log, slicing thinly.

2 Drill holes in the centre of the top and base and screw together, sinking the screw slightly and filling the hole with wood filler. Use a scrap of fabric to make a tablecloth.

3 To make a stool, cut a branch to the required height to fit the table.

4 To make a chair, cut a branch to the required height for a chair with back. Cut halfway across the branch at the right height for the chair seat (same height as stool). Cut neatly down the back of the chair to meet the seat cut. Neaten with a chisel.

5 To make a bed, cut two thin log slices for bed ends. On both, cut a straight edge so that they stand up. Glue a matchstick across the bottom of the inner face of each bed end for the bed section to rest on. Cut the bed base to the required length and glue in place. Use scraps of fabric to make bedding.

6 To make a lamp, cut a log slice for the base. Drill a hole in the base, using a drill bit that is the same diameter as your dowelling. Cut a length of dowelling and glue in place.

7 Make a shade by twisting a semicircle of thin card into a cone, gluing down the top edge. Put a small piece of adhesive putty on the top of the dowel and push on the shade.

8 Sand and oil all of the pieces with boiled linseed oil, rubbing them with a cloth once the oil has sunk in.

9 To make a peg doll, cut the bottom off a peg so the doll has legs to stand on. For a child doll, trim off the legs. Sand smooth.

10 Cut a scrap of felt to fit the adult doll. The length should measure from the neck (the indented area below the round head) to 1 cm (½ in) below the end of the 'legs'. The width needs to be 1 cm (½ in) wider than the diameter of the neck at the top, plus 2.5 cm (1 in) at the bottom. To dress the child doll, simply glue strips of fabric onto the body.

11 Sew the side seam of the adult doll's dress to form a tube and insert the peg. Sew a loose gathering stitch around the neck end of the felt and pull tight. Stitch to secure.

12 To provide stability, turn up the hem of the dress until it is even with the base of the peg and stitch in place. Stitch a shawl over the top of the felt dress.

13 Glue bits of knitting yarn on for the hair and draw the features of a simple face using pencil crayons.

Felt fishing set

Many children have never been fishing or even watched the boats in the harbour bringing in a catch. Have you ever taken your child to an aquarium to see the different shapes and colours of the fish? What a treat, if you could arrange for her to experience one of these activities. She will imitate what she has seen and use her imagination to extend this into play.

TEACH YOUR CHILD TO FISH

People have fished for food for many thousands of years. Once you show your child how to fish, she will find it a natural activity. Demonstrate how to lower the line gently into the water (which could simply be a blue muslin cloth spread out on the floor), as swinging the rod over her shoulder as fly fishermen do could be hazardous. To catch a fish requires skill, as the rod magnet has to make contact with the fish in order to lift it up and swing it into a waiting basket. As your child becomes more skilful, she will enjoy trying to catch more

than one fish at a time to end up with a basket full of fish of different sizes, shapes and colours.

Before you make the fish, try to look at some real ones, perhaps by visiting a fish stockist or a local garden centre where fish are displayed in tanks, or consult a book with illustrations. This will give you ideas for different shapes and colours. It is fun to decorate your fish with shiny stitching or sequins, to match the shining and sparkling of live fish in the water.

PLAYTIME

Make more than one rod so your toddler can fish with friends. Her imagination will be stretched as she and her friends make boats from upturned tables, surrounded by a sea of blue cloths with fish swimming all around. Hang baskets from cords stretched between the table legs for your toddler to slide from one end of the boat to the other as she sorts the fish. She may throw some fish back into the sea, ready to be caught again. This game will extend further as your child grows older and she begins to use her imagination to sail to far-off lands, bringing her catch back to the shore and selling it to the local shop, which can be set up in another part of the room. Perhaps she will meet some pirates on the way. This game has infinite possibilities and provides many wonderful ways for children to interact with each other.

Hints and tips

- You can use thin, strong branches instead of dowelling for the fishing rods.
- Use differently coloured cord for the fishing lines, so that each child can have her own.
- Use blue cloth to make a pool.
- Make fish in a range of colours, shapes and sizes.
- Provide baskets into which your child can drop the caught fish.
- Ensure washers are firmly attached to both the fish and the rods.
- Make sure your smaller washers are steel and not aluminium, which is not magnetic.

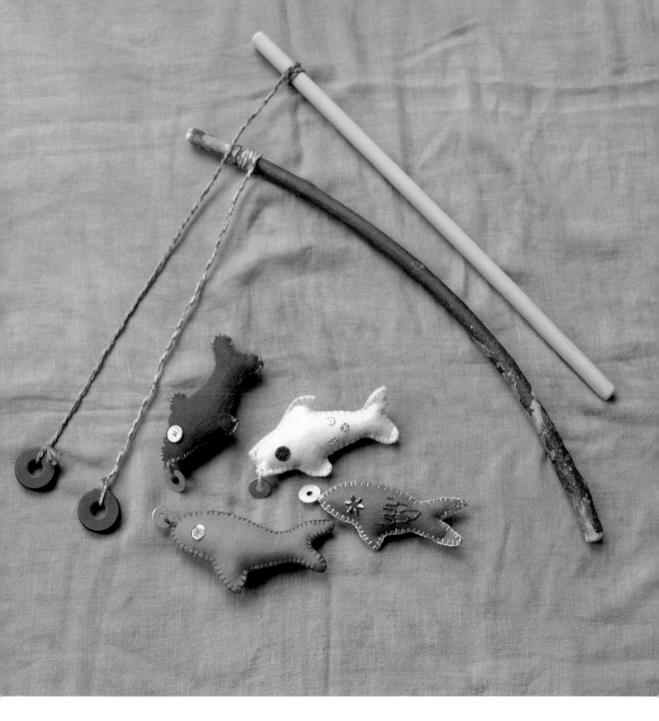

'*The most effective kind of education is that a child should play amongst lovely things.*'

Plato

Making a fishing set

This game takes considerable skill, so is recommended for children of three years and over. Smaller children may find it difficult to master, which could end in tears of frustration.

You will need

Pencil

Strong felt

Sharp scissors

Sequins

Sewing needle

Sewing thread

Embroidery needle

Embroidery thread

Carded, unspun
   sheep's wool*

1.5 cm (¾ in) diameter
   steel washers

Thin seasoned branches
   or 1 cm (½ in)
   diameter dowelling

Saw

Sandpaper

Craft knife

Cord for hanging

PVA glue

3 cm (1¼ in) diameter
   magnetic washers

*Tease unspun sheep's wool before use, pulling gently to separate dense fibres. A comb-like hand 'carder' speeds up the process.

How to do it

1 Draw a design for your fish on folded felt and cut out to give you two identical shapes. Vary the size and shape of your fish as you make more.

2 Sew on sequins or buttons as eyes and embroider other decorations, then stitch together each pair using blanket stitch (see page 28). Leave a small opening for stuffing.

3 Stuff softly with unspun sheep's wool, then sew the hole closed. Sew a steel washer firmly to the mouth area.

4 To make each rod, use a thin seasoned branch about 33 cm (13 in) long or trim a length of dowelling to size. Sand the ends of the branch or length of dowelling well.

5 Use a craft knife to score each branch or length of dowelling about 3 cm (1¼ in) in from one end. Tie a length of cord around the notch and glue in place to stop it slipping off.

6 Tie a magnetic washer tightly to the loose end of the cord.

Crowns and cloaks

Dressing up is tremendous fun for children of all ages and there are endless possibilities for imaginative play with a selection of crowns, cloaks, fairy wings and play cloths. Play is often stimulated by external circumstances and while children tend to imitate what they see first hand, they also use their imagination to stretch what they have already absorbed.

STIMULATING IMAGINATIVE PLAY

Up to age three, toddlers interact enthusiastically with their surroundings but they also want to stay close to the mother, father or carer, working or playing alongside the adult. They slowly venture to play alongside other children, but are still primarily concerned with their own self – finding out what the body is capable of and becoming more aware of the will impulse to 'do it myself'.

Between the ages of three and five, however, children develop new faculties, those of memory and imagination. They instinctively begin to transform things from their surroundings, using them in ways that are different from their original purpose. They see an object that stimulates a memory and their imagination begins to work. In order to play imaginatively in this way, children need to have seen or experienced a situation already and, at this age, that usually means building on domestic activities in the home and perhaps memorable one-off events such as a wedding or a holiday.

A favourite storybook might also trigger such play. Children love having stories read to them and looking at picture books, many of which contain pictures of fairies, princes and princesses – the perfect inspiration for dressing up. Golden crowns and cloaks make little boys feel quite kingly and little princesses love any pink or colourful fabric that they can wrap around themselves. Such elements bring a different dimension to a child's play, transforming him from himself and allowing him to become 'the other'.

TOOLS OF MAKE-BELIEVE

You can cut small squares of muslin or silk, dyed in plain colours, to make headdresses or to wrap around a child's neck and tie by two corners in the front to make a cloak. Slightly larger cloths can be wrapped around the waist to form dresses that hang to the floor. Other ways of wearing a square of muslin include tying it around the body like a sari or sarong, or tying a corner to each wrist to make wings. If making wings, it helps to attach the

Hints and tips

- Use differently coloured fabrics for cloaks.
- Choose thick, strong felt that does not fray.
- For simple headbands, plait lengths of carded wool and knot to size.
- Encourage your child to find other uses for the squares, perhaps as a pool for the fishing set (page 62) or a field for the felt horses (page 36).

fabric at the back to the collar of a shirt or dress to give the wings more shape.

You should always hem the fabric properly and keep it folded carefully in a basket when not in use. You can buy dyed muslin very cheaply at most haberdashery or fabric shops or you can buy soft material or silk scarves from secondhand shops and cut them up. Find colours and natural fabrics that appeal to the senses, choosing plain colours that are not too bright.

Making crowns and cloaks

These muslin squares are the simplest of dressing-up clothes.
If desired, cut extra squares of coloured cloth for a headdress to
drape over your child's head under the crown.

How to do it

You will need

Coloured muslin

Dressmaking scissors

Pins

Sewing needle

Sewing thread

Felt

PVA glue

Sequins

Coloured knitting yarn

Elastic, 1 cm (½ in) wide

Embroidery needle

Coloured embroidery
  thread

1 To make cloaks and headdresses, cut
1 metre (40 in) and 50 cm (20 in) squares
from the muslin. Hem on all sides and iron.

2 To make a crown, decide on your
preferred shape for the front section and
cut to size from a strip of folded felt.

3 Sew or glue decorations onto one side,
using offcuts of felt, sequins and coloured
knitting yarn knotted into flowers.

4 Cut a piece of elastic that will be the right
size for a child's head when attached to the
crown. Insert the ends between the two
pieces of felt and pin in place.

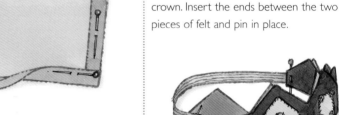

5 Stitch the two pieces of felt together, using
blanket stitch (see page 28) and coloured
embroidery thread. Remove the pins.

Interaction

Interaction

Children develop social skills through play. This is not only important for them as individuals but for society as a whole, for we cannot expect social cohesion among adults if we do not practise it when young. Children actively seek interaction with others.

Learning social skills

Children play 'alongside' in their second year and they play 'with' in their third year. This develops into more organized play in their fourth year. An invitation to participate should be taken with the respect it deserves.

Children can be obstreperous, annoying, calculating, manipulative and sometimes even cruel. While adults have, at least in theory, the potential to work on themselves, children and young people need adult help to change. Social skills are learnt through social contact. Achieving the vision of a better world means starting young: 'If we are to reach real peace in the world, we shall have to begin with children', as Gandhi put it. Our communities are formed by explicit or implicit consent and it is unfair for a child to grow up without being made aware of what is expected of her and how to arrive there. Play is more than just cultural transmission, of course, yet it does contain elements of shared perspectives and values.

Intrusive technologies

If you want your child to develop good social skills, be wary of television, DVDs and video games. Like all technologies these have their place, but not necessarily in early childhood. Just as we change the world for better or ill through our technology,

Research on electronic media

Recent research has backed concerns about the effect on children of excessive television viewing, finding, for example, that speedily shifting images may abnormally stimulate the brain. The American Academy of Paediatrics now recommends that there should be no television at all for children under two years of age and cites over 1,000 studies that 'point overwhelmingly to a causal connection between media violence and aggressive behaviour in children'. Studies reported in 2007 in the *New Scientist* have shown that video games increase social aggression, and a 2006 report by Britain's National Children's Bureau highlights that very young children 'do become more aggressive after either playing or watching a violent video game. Such evidence suggests that children (at least in the short term) copy or mimic what they have seen on the screen.'

so technology changes our consciousness. Electronic media are both intrusive and powerful.

Children invariably find ways to occupy themselves if left to it and periods of inactivity can be fruitful. Avoid giving into the temptation to suggest watching television. The constant wish to be entertained can become an addiction, with attempts no longer made to explore ones own

resources. This is hardly right for the young child, who should be moving physically for the sake of her future health, developing her learning skills and exploring the world of fantasy and imagination. In the early years, a child needs primarily to lay down the foundations for her literacy skills, gain direct experience of common human values, enhance her communication skills, develop the will to overcome frustrations and engage with people in all their complexity. Placing your child in front of the television denies her the opportunity of fulfilling these needs.

Television watching for young children should be a family activity, where it is monitored for suitability and discussed so programmes can be put in context and limited. It is hard to undo the

negative effects of putting a television set in your child's bedroom.

Interactive 'edu-tainment' may help certain children with disabilities including learning disabilities and attention problems, and of course it can be fun. But, as for children in general, this technology needs careful assessment and control. In most situations, simple toys given with your time, patience and love will prove more effective.

This view about the dangers of electronic media does not stem from a misplaced vision of a 'golden age' of childhood, nor is it an allergic response to the modern world. Instead, it arises from the experience of Steiner teachers who have worked with six-year-olds who could not play and had to be taught the elements of their own childhood. These teachers also saw the later consequences in the classroom. The electronic babysitter contains risks for your family life, so treat with care.

The elements of social play

The schema, or conceptual pattern, of play is much debated and, in many ways, remains unclear, as a child can readily move from one form to another.

Nevertheless, providing ourselves with certain categories, with the proviso that they are not definitive, can be helpful. Child development is increasingly viewed as interpersonal as well as intrapersonal. In social play, to which children also bring their individual characteristics, we can observe forms such as 'parallel', 'onlooker' and 'cooperative' play. Playing in any of these modes with your child will give you the opportunity to view the world from her point of view. She will feel you are giving her your full attention, helping her to build an enduring relationship. You will also learn to communicate more effectively with her. Children who are less verbally inclined can express emotions and thoughts through play.

At two years of age, in what is sometimes called symbolic play, a child can give life to her dolls. She allows the doll to perform actions, like drinking tea, which she has seen and now imitates. She is in the process of developing from a state where, according to Steiner, 'children are mainly interested in their own body, they do not regard the outer world but possess just a dreamlike consciousness, of being enclosed in a sphere, which really takes in the effects of the outer world as pictures', to a state in which she can also collaborate with others and adjust her behaviour in play to achieve simple goals. She communicates using brief verbal statements and facial and limb gestures.

From the age of three, children can begin to conceive that other minds exist, can gradually comprehend the behaviour and intentions of others and can play games of shared pretend with a shared focus. In play they can progressively moderate their behaviour to accommodate others in their group and by four and five years old are extremely sensitive to each other. They can also influence the feelings of others intentionally.

The world weaver

At this stage play contains narrative and meanings. When a child is engaged in this, she becomes a 'world weaver' – producing a paradoxical space where the child understands the difference between reality and fantasy, but simultaneously the fantasy is based on reality. She can be explicit about pretending and recognize it in others. In the words of the poet, Coleridge, it is 'a suspension of disbelief'. She is able to define play for herself and that is simply part of being a child.

We should remember that playing with peers is not the same as playing with adults and the child will develop different strategies. Adults tend to seek goals, whereas a child's peers can be imaginative or exploratory without such pressure. This allows for unusual or insightful solutions to unforeseen problems. Time is of a different dimension and motivation comes from other sources. A child and her peers can, together, disassociate from the representation of the world given by the senses and find new universes. The physical activity they generate together has a positive effect on growth and neurological development. As parents, we should try to ensure a good balance between family interaction, interaction with peers and solitary play.

Daily rest

Young children are the most physically active people in society and play occupies most of their waking hours. By four years of age the child has doubled her birth length, although the growth rate between two and four represents only half the gain of the first two years. A child's body is supple enough to deal with minor falls and her agility results in the speedy development of motor skills and an increasing enjoyment of her prowess. This mobility builds up organs, such as the brain, with the cerebral cortex being completely developed by the age of four. Energy expended on social activity also has its demands, and the consequences go beyond tiredness caused by physical exertion. The practice of sympathy, empathy and mimesis also requires intensive input. Children need quiet time during which they interact within themselves to 'digest' the day's experiences. Good sleeping rhythms also refresh the child so she can then play intensively. It is therefore advisable to give your child a habitual time for a daily rest.

Trust in the world

A child can give herself up totally to certain situations and has a natural deep trust in others. In *The Foundations of Human Experience*, a series of teacher-training lectures given at the first Steiner Waldorf school in 1919, Steiner suggested that this was a form of devotion. Devotion is a state of reaching an understanding, not through intellectual analysis and scientific insights, which in a way distance us, but by letting things enter your soul. This openness shows how a child trusts the world and, unless taught otherwise by bitter experience or negative intervention, sees it as good.

This giving over of oneself manifests itself in imitation, but is also a key as to how children play with each other. Such a mood means the child at first sees the loving adults around her as perfect; although later our imperfections become more apparent to her. This is interaction on another level. Steiner further suggests that if children are brought up in this mood they will, much later as mature adults, be able to bring spiritual beneficence to others too, because they have developed an inner source of reverence.

Finger puppets

We spend hours with our children, talking to them and doing or making things with them. For the most part this interaction is habitual and therefore unconscious, without us necessarily paying attention to how we move, sound or act. Neither are we likely to be aware of the effect we have on our children through this interaction.

When children interact with each other, they are even less conscious of their actions and toddlers in particular have no awareness yet of the impression or effect they might have on another child. To become conscious of our interactions with our children means that we must be 'in the moment' at all times, truly present in everything we say or do. This is quite a task for busy parents, but so worthwhile if you make the effort. Playing simple games, telling stories or singing with your toddler make good starting points, and it is wonderful when you see the joy in a child's response to you. Ten minutes of conscious play – of 'being there' for your toddler – is infinitely more valuable than an hour of 'just being around'!

PLAYING WITH FINGER PUPPETS

Using these simple finger puppets as a form of interaction allows you to make up stories, talk directly to a puppet on your toddler's finger and even to sing or tell stories. Perform a show for toddlers using finger puppets and the response will be overwhelming. Children are always totally engrossed in a story. If you approach a puppet directly, as if it is real, toddlers will too and you will awaken their imagination. You can also use the puppets to perform the actions of a nursery rhyme, such as this one:

Two little dicky birds sitting on a wall,
One named Peter and one named Paul
Fly away Peter, fly away Paul
Come back Peter, come back Paul.

Alternatively, use the puppets to tell a story – perhaps a mummy bird talking to her baby bird about taking its first flight from the nest, flying around the room and back again. Puppetry helps expand imaginative play and provides an incentive for interaction. As your toddler begins to interact with other children more directly, he will want to make up puppet shows with them. Creating a family of birds that can sit on the branches of a tree, or in a little wool nest balancing on the branch, will promote your toddler's communication skills, helping him to acquire the language he needs for telling a story of his own.

Hints and tips
- Make different sizes of puppet to fit fingers of both parent and child.
- Use different colour combinations for interest.
- Make different designs – a dog, cat or rabbit.
- Make people using the basic design for standing puppets (page 80) adapted to fit the finger.

Making finger puppets

The puppets must fit snugly onto the finger without slipping off during play, so make them in two different sizes – larger for you, smaller for your toddler.

How to do it

You will need

Tracing paper

Pencil

Felt in a range of colours

Pins

Dressmaking scissors

PVA glue

Embroidery needle

Embroidery thread

Carded, unspun
 sheep's wool*

* Tease unspun sheep's wool before use, pulling gently to separate dense fibres. A comb-like hand 'carder' speeds up the process.

1 Draw a bird outline on tracing paper, as shown in the illustration below. The finished size should fit a finger, so should be no more than 8 cm (3¼ in) in height for a child and 10 cm (4 in) for an adult.

2 Pin the patterns to coloured felt, folded double so that you cut two of each shape.

3 For a large puppet, cut out felt circles for eyes and glue them in place. For a smaller bird, simply create the eyes with a few stitches of embroidery thread.

4 Draw patterns for the inner and outer wings on tracing paper, pin to folded felt and cut out two inner wings and two outer wings. Glue each small wing in position on a large wing and then glue the wings onto the two sides of the bird.

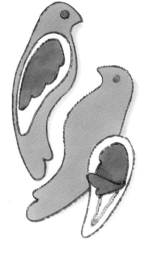

5 Oversew (see page 39) the two bird sides together, leaving a gap for inserting a finger in the tail section.

6 Stuff the head lightly with wool to give it some shape.

7 If you would like to make other animal puppets, try creating templates following these simple designs (below). Redraw to the size of your child's finger.

Standing puppets

In giving your child the simplest of toys you give her a chance to create a world of her own. A pine cone might become a pig; a bit of wool, a little lamb; a stone, a mouse. This creativity, encouraged by leaving your child free to develop her memory and imagination, will emerge in later years when she becomes open-minded and adaptable.

PLAY BASED ON OBSERVATION

Standing puppets are a useful addition to your toddler's collection of toys, for she will use them in many different ways. To begin with, you can spend time interacting with your toddler, making up stories involving everyday activities and using the puppets to re-enact what happens in daily life.

Your toddler soaks up what she sees, hears and touches, so that it becomes part of her. Therefore you need to make sure that what you provide for her in her environment is gentle, pure and true. If you move a puppet in a jerky way, for example, your child will imitate you. Not only will she make the same jerky movements with her puppet, but the movements may go so deeply into her being

that she begins to move in the same way herself. As you play with your toddler, you should become much more observant of what she absorbs from her environment. This will help you to make your own movements slower, more even and tranquil, to speak only when you really have something important to say and to sing with a gentle voice.

THE VALUE OF PUPPETRY

Puppetry appeals to all of the senses: it contains movement, colour and sound. You can start by making a simple scene and using the puppets to interact with your toddler. The next step is for you to produce a simple puppet show, using the puppets to re-enact a story, such as 'The Gingerbread Man' or the Brothers Grimm tale, 'The Turnip'. These stories are simple enough that your child can draw them from her picture memory and own imagination when performing puppet shows with her friends in later years.

Moving on, you could give each puppet a permanent identity and create a world for them, telling a different story about them each day. By doing this, you introduce the idea of characters and personalities developing as time goes on. Your toddler will extend the floor play by introducing animals, wooden blocks (see page 51), cloths and anything else to hand, when she plays with these puppets as she grows older.

Hints and tips

- Make male and female puppets by changing the hair.
- Add accessories that make each puppet different – a cloak or hat, for example.
- Make smaller puppets as children and a baby for the mother to carry in a sling.
- You could embroider or decorate the felt body before sewing it into a cylinder.
- You could draw facial features with pencil crayons rather than stitching them.

'Out of observation of a simple tabletop
puppet show, rich impulses can grow
for the child's own play.'

Bronja Zahlingen, *A Lifetime of Joy*

Making a standing puppet

Use this project to make a range of puppets of different sizes. You can make the measurements larger or smaller, but always keep the proportions roughly the same.

How to do it

You will need

Carded, unspun sheep's wool*

Knitting yarn

Sharp scissors

Skin-coloured cotton-knit fabric

Sewing needle

Sewing thread

Embroidery needle

Red and blue or brown embroidery thread

Pins (optional)

Coloured felt

Thin card

Hair-coloured carded, unspun sheep's wool*

Scraps of colourful fabric (optional)

* Tease unspun sheep's wool before use, pulling gently to separate dense fibres. A comb-like hand 'carder' speeds up the process.

1 Make a firm head for the puppet using unspun sheep's wool to form a tight ball, approximately 5 cm (2 in) in height. Wrap the ball in a rough square of unspun wool and tie off the excess with knitting yarn. Leave some excess wool hanging to give stability to the neck.

2 Wrap the head tightly in a square of skin-coloured cotton-knit fabric, with the grain of the fabric running vertically up and down the face. Overlap the edges at the back of the head, turn under the raw edge and sew a vertical seam.

3 Now pull the top edge of the skin-coloured fabric to the back of the head, turn under the raw edges and stitch neatly to secure. Tie a length of thread around the base of the head to form the neck, leaving some wool stuffing protruding.

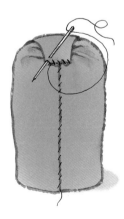

4 Stitch on the facial features using appropriately coloured embroidery thread. Keep them simple and use pins to act as guides for positioning, if desired (or simply draw on the features).

5 Make the body. Cut a piece of felt about 12 x 20 cm (5 x 8 in) and join the short edges to make a cylinder. Turn the cylinder inside out, so the seam is on the inside. Fold in the top edge of the felt cylinder, if necessary, and make a row of gathering stitches close to the top.

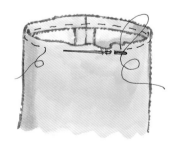

6 Draw up the gathering stitches and sew the body cylinder to the head at the neck.

7 Cut a small card disc to fit in the base of the cylinder and a slightly larger felt disc to fit on top of the card disc, to form the puppet's base.

8 Stuff the felt body with wool, without packing it in too firmly. Insert the small card disc and place the felt disc over the top, stitching it neatly to the felt cylinder.

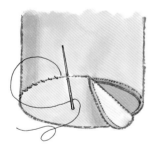

9 Stitch a tuft of unspun sheep's wool or knitting yarn onto the doll's head for hair and add additional clothes if you wish to dress the puppet, making them from scraps of coloured fabric.

Marionettes

Rudolf Steiner once said, even before the advent of television, that 'puppet shows are an antidote to the effects of modern civilization'. Watching television is a passive activity that often makes children overactive afterwards. However, when you act out a story for a toddler he remains calm and thoughtful, using his imagination to interpret what he sees in the show.

PERFORMING A SHOW

Telling a story while moving puppets is a skill that takes practice and will inspire your children with the impulse to do it as well. You can use another person alongside you to tell the story and provide music, or involve your child by letting him move the puppets while you narrate.

Marionettes are one step on from standing puppets (see page 80), as playing with them requires more nimble fingers and the dexterity that comes with practice and age. For this reason, they are most suitable for children of four years and up.

Hints and tips

- Use light, single-toned fabrics that flow as you move the puppet around.
- Consider which colours are suitable for your puppet characters. Keep fabrics plain, not patterned.
- For strings, use thread that will not twist or fray.
- For greater control of the hands, attach the stringing threads to the thumb side of the hands (not the tips of the fingers).
- Add crowns and jewellery to the puppets by sewing on additional fabric, card, sequins or other decorations. Keep it simple.

The ability to handle the puppets will come quite easily if you show your child how to do it properly first. Stringed puppets should flow in their movements, appearing to almost float above the cloth laid down as the ground beneath them. It is important that they remain 'on the ground' – neither dragging so that they look as if they are walking on their knees nor hovering above the ground like a bumblebee.

Having an adult visibly in control of the puppets is comforting and also provides an opportunity for the young child to imitate what you are doing. He see your mistakes and successes and is satisfied that you are in charge. Nothing that is done is hidden, and this gives your young child the confidence that he is able to do it, too. He absorbs the movements of the puppets and, when confident and skilful enough, will be able to replicate them himself. He will be so interested in what is happening in the story that your presence, your actions and your voice won't be a distraction.

POWER OF STORY-TELLING

Fairy tales and short stories that you can either memorize or invent yourself can centre on human encounters and experiences. Puppets will bring these scenarios to life for your toddler. He will sit, quietly absorbed, and follow the scene as it unfolds. If the figures are simply made, with

colours suitable for the different characters, your toddler's creative powers will be engaged and his imagination will begin to work on the story. At the right age your toddler will come to copy these themes on his own.

Silk is an ideal fabric from which to make these marionettes, as it has a floating quality. It won't catch on the items or toys that make up the scene, especially if it has been properly hemmed. You can also use muslin, if preferred. Keep the colours soft and plain if possible. When it comes to drawing on the face, remember to keep the features simple so that a puppet can take on any expression your child wants it to have.

Making a simple marionette

You can make this puppet quickly and easily from light, single-toned fabrics that flow as you move the puppet. Consider using light muslin, silk and satin-type fabrics, such as old silk scarves.

How to do it

You will need

Carded, unspun sheep's wool *

Skin-coloured cotton-knit fabric

Dressmaking scissors

Light, solid-coloured silky fabric

Sewing needle

Sewing thread

Small flat pebbles

Thin nylon thread

1 To make the head and body, take a 20 cm (8 in) square of unspun sheep's wool and roll it into a sausage shape. Cut a 22 cm (9 in) piece of skin-coloured fabric.

2 Wrap the skin-coloured fabric very tightly around the unspun sheep's wool, stitching firmly up the back of the puppet. Secure behind the head and at the body base. Tie off the neck tightly to create a head about 7 cm (3 in) long, pushing folds to the back.

3 To make the main garment, cut a 45 × 45 cm (18 × 18 in) square of silky fabric, fold it on the bias and hem the edges.

*Tease unspun sheep's wool before use, pulling gently to separate dense fibres. A comb-like hand 'carder' speeds up the process.

4 Cut a central V shape in the fold, big enough for the head to fit through. Run a gathering stitch around the neck opening, draw it tight and sew it firmly around the neck. Turn back the 'sleeves' to arm length and sew the ends to the neck underneath.

5 To make the hands, cover two small pebbles with small pieces of skin-coloured fabric and tie off the wrists. Sew the hands firmly to the ends of the sleeves.

6 Cut two pieces of thread to a length of about 54 cm (22 in) and one piece to a length of about 35 cm (14 in). Attach the longer pieces to the wrists or stitch them to the thumb position. Stitch the third piece to the top of the head. Knot the three pieces together about 7 cm (3 in) from the ends, using the excess to create a hanging loop. When attaching the threads, check that the arms hang lower than shoulder height.

Moving pictures

There is nothing more peaceful, more engaging or more nourishing than spending time telling stories to your child. She loves this intimate interaction, your undivided attention and the story you are telling. Moving pictures provide an opportunity for you to stretch your imagination, while enlivening that of your toddler.

STORIES ABOUT YOUR CHILD

'Reading the pictures' is the first step in literacy, and will lead naturally to reading the words when your toddler is ready. Your toddler loves nothing more than listening to stories about herself: she is the centre of her world and therefore everything else revolves around her. Begin by making up stories about everyday activities and events that happen to your toddler. She will be fascinated to hear you retell the events of the day for instance, especially if you find a quiet time in which to do so. Sitting still after a busy morning or at bedtime brings a peaceful mood to whatever is to come (hopefully sleep!). Building a quiet time of sharing stories together into the rhythm of your day is beneficial to you both.

USING PICTURES TO TELL A STORY

Rudolf Steiner said that a child needs pictures that can move. He felt that this was a good way of transforming the inanimate image into a representation of living action. Making a simple moving picture for your toddler provides you with the opportunity to invent anew continuously, finding inspiration through daily activities and transforming them into stories for your toddler to enjoy.

Simple representations in the picture are enough: there need be no words to distract her, just pictures containing characters that can move. Once you have made one simple picture, such as the boat on the sea, any story can begin to unfold. Where is the boat coming from? Where is it going? What adventures are the characters that live on this boat having as they sail from their home?

With a young child, it is always important to include a lot of repetition in a story. A story should have a beginning and an end, which is satisfying in itself. It should possibly contain a song or a rhyme, which your child will learn through constant repetition. The story, too, should be told over and over again, perhaps even for a week or more before

---

Hints and tips

- If using printed card, draw your design on paper and glue to the card.
- You can cut pictures from magazines to glue onto the background.
- Rounding the corners of the finished picture gives it its own frame.
- This method can be adapted to make simple greetings cards.
- Make sure your toddler can move all of the pieces freely, widening the slots if necessary.

it is expanded to include another event or happening, but always with the same ending. It is no surprise that 'once upon a time' and 'happily ever after' are so well remembered.

DEVELOPING A THEME
Your picture can change as you grow more adventurous and you can cut out more characters to use. The picture of the house is archetypal – all children live somewhere – so this offers a certain security for your toddler. And who lives in or near the house? Why, *she* does, or her friends, or the little animals, birds and creatures who come to visit. Using a range of characters in the cut-out spaces will keep her engaged and entertained in a peaceful and gentle way as she moves them about.

Making moving pictures

Use the right movements, such as moving the rabbit up and down if hopping and from side to side if running. You can adapt the pictures, changing the boat for a duck and so on.

How to do it

1 To make a house picture, paint or colour the background and round off the corners.

2 Draw your pop-up additions on card, giving each a tag long enough to protrude beyond the bottom edge of the picture.

3 Cut slots in the main picture for the tags of the pop-up additions, and insert the tags from the front of the picture to the back.

4 Secure the tags in place with paper, glued at the ends only, to stop the pop-up additions slipping out of the picture.

5 To add a circular feature, draw and cut out a complete circle with a long tag and colour as desired. Cut out a section from the main background with a craft knife, making sure it is less than half a circle and that it will not interfere with the centre point of the circular feature after assembly.

6 Decide which way the circular feature will move, then mark the back of the main picture to enable you to cut a slot for the tag, making it slightly wider than the tag.

7 Push a drawing pin (thumb tack) through the front of the main picture and circular feature. Secure with an earring butterfly clip.

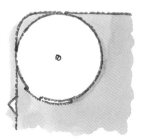

8 To make a boat picture, paint or draw a seascape on a sheet of card.

9 Draw and colour a boat approximately 8 cm (3¼ in) wide with a long tag. The tag should hang some 2 cm (¾ in) below the bottom of the finished picture. Draw and colour a fish. Cut out both fish and boat.

10 Use the craft knife to cut two slots in the seascape for the boat's tag. The first needs to be high enough to allow the boat to ride the waves, up to 8 cm (3¼ in) wide and wave-shaped. Cut the second slot 5 cm (2 in) down from the first and central to it. It should be a little wider than the tag.

11 Thread the tag from the front of the picture to the back through the upper slot and bring it from the back to the front of the picture through the second slot.

12 Now glue the fish to the visible part of the tag, approximately 2 cm (¾ in) below the lower slot. Move the tag from side to side to waggle the boat.

Wooden pull train

Making things with your toddler is always lots of fun and creating this simple little train is no exception. Right from the beginning you can involve him in the creative process by taking him out into nature to find just the right branch for the train and another smaller one for the funnel. Hunting for materials is a wonderful activity to do together.

WORKING TOGETHER

Find out if the train branch is the right size by wrapping your hand around it – if the fingers meet, it's perfect. It needs to be straight too, so roll it along the ground to check for bumps. Is the wood strong enough or have little creatures been gnawing at it? Is the bark smooth or rough? Will it peel off or does it look shiny enough to stay there forever? Asking these questions will bring you a new perception and spirit of discovery that will soon transfer to your toddler. Nature is a wonderful teacher if only we open our eyes to it.

Your toddler can help you with all the stages of building this train, because they are so simple. Let him watch you rhythmically saw the log, then let

him hold the saw with your hands around his as you keep the rhythm going. This song can be adapted to any very simple tune:

> We're sawing, we're sawing, we're sawing
>   all day long
> We're sawing, we're sawing, and singing a sawing
>   song.

You can change the words to suit the activity, such as drilling, sanding or polishing. Your toddler will get into the rhythm of the song and of the activity itself, as you keep time to the song.

PLAYTIME

All little children love trains. Experiencing a real steam train – seeing the driver with his flag and the smoke coming out the chimney, hearing the sound of the whistle and the rhythmic puff puff of the engine – is a sensory delight for them and really enlivens their play. Creating tracks and bridges made from planks and blocks (see page 51), and running the tracks between fields made from cloths and a mountain made from cushions, will all add to the potential of the scene. Left alone with some little friends, your toddler will begin to explore not only the possibilities of this play, but also those of interaction with his peers.

Hints and tips

- Make sure your wood is dry and well seasoned or it will crack once cut (see page 51).
- Adapt the same instructions to make a longer trailer with four wheels.
- If using peg dolls (see page 61) as passengers, cut them shorter to fit into the trailer.
- Make sure the branches are smooth and round; you can leave the bark on if it is even and smooth.

'Play is the road to childhood happiness and adult brilliance.'

Joseph Chilton Pearce

Making a wooden train

Make as many carriages as you wish, either to carry passengers or freight. For example, you could make a log carriage to transport straight twigs that you have collected. Cut them to size and tie them neatly onto the log carriage.

How to do it

1 First cut out all your pieces. Saw a 7 cm (3 in) piece of wood from the larger diameter branch for the train engine. Trim the front end at a slight diagonal. Cut a 5 cm (2 in) piece of wood from the same branch and saw in half lengthways, to create the wheelhouse and the body of the carriage. Cut wheels from the larger branch, each about 5 mm (¼ in) thick. You will need four for the engine and an additional two for each carriage that you make.

2 Glue the flat edge of one half, standing upright, to the back end of the engine.

3 Cut a 2 cm (¾ in) length from the smaller diameter branch for the funnel. Drill a hole in the top of the engine, equal in diameter to that of the funnel, about 5 mm (¼ in) down. Glue the funnel in place.

4 If you want to make a seat for a passenger, such as the peg child on page 61, use a pencil to mark the circumference of the hole, then drill.

5 Drill through the train engine to make two holes for the dowels that will hold the two pairs of wheels, about one-third up from the bottom of the branch. Measure the space so that both sets of wheels will fit on the train front without touching each other. Do the same for the single set of wheels on each carriage. Make sure that the drill bit measures at least 2 mm (⅛ in) bigger than the diameter of your dowelling.

6 Drill a hole in the centre of each wheel that is equal in diameter to that of your dowelling. It needs to fit tightly.

7 Now cut two pieces of dowel for the engine, measuring approximately 5 cm (2 in) and an additional length for each carriage. Check that they are long enough to pass through the train and both wheels and washers.

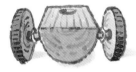

8 Sand all pieces of wood. Glue one wheel to a dowel, add a washer, pass the dowel through the train, add another washer and fit the second wheel, checking it spins easily before gluing it in place. Repeat for the other pairs of wheels.

9 Oil all of the pieces of wood with boiled linseed oil, rubbing the excess off with a cloth, before attaching hook and eye screws to connect the engine to the carriage(s).

Discovery

Discovery

Different cultures appreciate play in different ways. The Western work ethic has tended to disregard its value, at least ostensibly, although, in fact, the industry of adult 'play' – sport and leisure – takes up greater resources and time then ever before. Football and the Olympic Games attract international interest. These activities, along with watching plays, playing music and reading novels, are all, in a cultural sense, play.

Joyful knowledge

In some cultures adult games are not seen as purely recreational pursuits. Games of the Kalapalo people of the Amazon rainforest, for example, have underlying mythological and cosmological meanings. Their content reflects ritually social life, oral tradition and the physical skills needed for survival, and adds to the cognitive and cultural development of each individual. The games are used to reveal purposes and explain the world the Kalapalo encounter. It is what the anthropologist Pierre Clastres called *gai savoir* – joyful knowledge. Children also have a propensity to learn this way, as Walt Whitman wrote in his poem:

> *There was a child went forth every day*
> *And the first object he looked on, that he became*
> *And that object became part of him for the day or*
> *   a certain part of the day*
> *Or for many years or stretching cycles of years.'*

Adults use games to make new discoveries beyond the everyday; children use games to discover the everyday. In his second and third years, having by now developed a basis for his thinking and 75 per cent of his brain, the child begins to extend his capacity for thought out into the world. He enters an age of discovery. As Steiner wrote in *The World of the Sense and the World of the Spirit*: 'It is absolutely essential that, before we begin to think, before we so much as begin to set our thinking in motion, we experience the condition of wonder.' We embark on voyages into new, exciting and unknown territory having exercised and strengthened our senses, and wonder still accompanies us on our travels. In a way it is all a dream and that is why, as adults, we forget these early experiences so readily. But as our 'self' begins to define itself, so we are more able to retain our memories and can start creating mental maps that guide us. Consequently the period from three years onwards has been called the 'age of fantasy'.

Perceived risk

Discovery and creativity involve risk. When going beyond our normal boundaries there are no guidelines about what we might find. In affluent Western societies we are becoming risk-averse with regard to childhood and these adult fears can severely restrict a child's movements and reduce

Nature deficit disorder

Young children are often corralled from home to daycare and then back home again, with a 'useful' schedule of guided activities and skill acquisition inserted into an already breathless routine. With the metropolitan lifestyle increasingly practised around the world, it is becoming more difficult to find play spaces for children that include any natural habitat or wildness. The term 'nature deficit disorder' has been coined to describe how children are becoming removed from direct experience of nature, unfortunately to their detriment.

Children need to be given time and space to breathe inwardly. Children love the natural world and it is the place where some of their deeply impressive discoveries are made. This becomes increasingly important as the child grows. The spiritual qualities of nature speak directly to a child's soul. It is not always easy for parents to rectify a lack of nature and providing such accessible spaces becomes more a community responsibility. Interestingly, there is clear evidence from the Netherlands that the crime rate goes down in communities providing better play spaces for their children. There is a case here for parent solidarity in defining new and child-friendly neighbourhood policies. In Sweden, too, it has been found that communities working together on improving facilities for children feel that they have improved everybody's lifestyle.

Following a child's desire to discover nature is therefore one way of finding social cohesiveness. At home, you can bring your observations of nature into the games you play, reminding your child of what he has seen, felt and experienced. The bird in the bush or a rabbit in the field can become the toy animal in his hand; the respect he shows it is an echo of respect and love for the natural world in general.

the possibility of him making his own discoveries. Contrary to the impression often given by the media, the world is no more dangerous than it was, arguably less so. Yet today children have fewer opportunities to play together and some schools are reducing, even prohibiting, playtime owing to perceived risks. The consequences for a child are lack of exercise, less confidence in physical ability, increased anxiety, withdrawal of initiative and a paucity of opportunities to discover for himself.

The child's right to freedom to discover and the natural protective sensibility of parenthood are no easy bedfellows. As parents we have to struggle to find where the healthy balance lies. Playing with your child can give you confidence in his abilities, which can encourage you to give him the freedom to experience the joys of childhood to the full. At this age, if given opportunities for self-education, a child can learn much more than through externally imposed educational programmes. He should continue to experience the wholeness of the world. There is enough time to unpick and dissect it later in primary, secondary and tertiary education.

Discovery for all

In 1932, after years of close and caring observation, Susan Isaacs, the great English early years' pioneer, pinpointed three modes of play in early childhood: love of movement and perfecting bodily skills; interest in actual things and events (the discovery of the world without); and delight in make-believe (the expression of the world within). These correlate well with Steiner's tripartite view of the human being as will (doing), thought and feeling. Although no single play activity operates exclusively in any of these areas, they all play a greater or lesser role in whatever the child is doing. When playing with the wind wands on page 106, for example, your child will delight in the discovery of wind blowing through the ribbons at the same time as he exercises his own body in running. Playing with the boats on page 110 in water will submerge him in the natural world and at the same time he will exercise both mind and body as he re-enacts a favourite story. As adults, we can observe which capacity is coming to the fore and help the child integrate all three in order eventually to balance them himself, as he will increasingly need to do as he grows older.

This book emphasizes the relevance of Steiner's insights, and those of many others, concerning the benefits of play for children. Steiner was able to put deep spiritual insights into inspiring language and concepts that can be expanded and developed further to fit the questions of our own times.

Playing with your child is the meeting of your purpose and the child's nature. Both your child and you can contribute to this meeting and, in so doing, combine the spiritual purpose of the child with what is, albeit often hidden, in your own nature. This is the realm of discovery for all. Discoveries are not just made with new thoughts but also with new eyes. The bright open eyes of a child in wonder can be your inner eyes of discovery through the means of being at one with him.

Some of this philosophical approach may seem a long way from making simple games and playing creatively with your child. But, by allowing such thoughts to live in you, you will find another level of relating to your child that will encourage and sustain you when the problems and responsibilities of parenthood appear taxing or overwhelming. There is no such thing as a perfect parent, however high-minded and devoted we think we are. It is the interaction between parent and child, as well as child and child that brings results. By concentrating on the relationships, we work spiritually. We allow each child to participate in the relationship, which he is perfectly able to do, encouraging this by acknowledging his competence in this domain. As Steiner wrote: 'All that child enjoys must live and be as though it were her own nature.'

By working with appreciation and love, we creatively develop the emotional connection between human beings. By playing with your child, and letting your play be child-led, you can fill it with what the child needs from you. Nor are you alone. A child can lead us into realms that are beyond our normal nature, helping us to become better parents, and better individuals too.

Parachute people

Children come to know the four ancient elements of earth, air, water and fire through their play, as they discover the delights of nature. Many of the toys in this chapter are connected to the elements and, as she plays with them, your toddler will begin to discover not only the world around her, but also what happens to her toys when touched by one of the elements and how much influence these elements have on her daily life.

AT ONE WITH NATURE

Children love to splash in all types of water, from puddles to the sea. They will dig in earth, sand, stones and clay, and play with mud when earth and water mix. Children enjoy sitting beside a fire in the hearth or watching a candle flame flicker, and they are fascinated by the wind, being attracted by anything that floats in the air: the dust dancing in a sunbeam, a butterfly fluttering above a flower, a feather caught by a breeze or the different shapes, sizes and colours of the clouds moving in the sky. You can play with the element of air simply by watching the way seeds fall from sycamore trees, spiralling downwards and finally coming to rest upright in the earth below, or the way they are blown from dandelions and other flowerheads.

Anything you do outside in nature that requires active movement on the part of your toddler is healthy for her, not only for her physical growth but also to develop a good sense of balance and confidence in what her body can accomplish.

PARACHUTE PLAY

The concept of flying is a joyful one for young children and yours will love to watch parachute people as they drift gently down to earth only to be gathered up and thrown again. She will not yet have the strength or skill to throw her parachute person high enough, but you can do it for her. Take a few of them to the park or out into the garden and throw them into the air for her. They will float straight down or may be carried by the wind for your toddler to chase and catch before they land. When she is older, she may drop the toys from a tree she has climbed or throw them from a bridge.

Experiment with different sizes of chute and use short or long strings from which to hang different sizes of toy. You can make parachutes while out in a park or forest, using whatever you find around you. Your handkerchief, tied with a piece of string from your pocket, with a feather, leaf or twig hanging from it, can make a wonderful parachute. The possibilities are endless.

Hints and tips

- For a parachute, you can use an old silk scarf, a handkerchief or any light cotton fabric.
- If you use cotton, paint or draw on it to personalize it for your toddler.
- The lighter the person and the shorter the yarn strings, the better the parachute will float.

Making a parachute person

To throw the parachute, hold it by the centre of the silk canopy and drop from a height. Alternatively, crunch up the toy in your hand and throw it upwards. It will always float down.

How to do it

You will need

20 cm (8 in) muslin square or similar light fabric

Sewing needle

Sewing thread

Carded, unspun sheep's wool*

20 cm (8 in) silk square or thin cotton handkerchief

Strong cotton yarn

Sharp scissors

* Tease unspun sheep's wool before use, pulling gently to separate dense fibres. A comb-like hand 'carder' speeds up the process.

1 To make the parachutist, fold the muslin square in half and sew up the side seams.

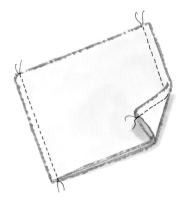

2 Turn the muslin right sides out and position a knotted length of unspun sheep's wool for the head as shown in the illustration. Tie tightly with thread to secure the head.

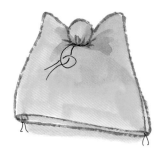

3 Lightly stuff the corners to make arms and legs and the middle area to make the body. Sew up the bottom seam, gathering the fabric to shape the legs, and secure with a few stitches.

4 Give shape to the arms by gathering them in around the waist and securing with a few stitches. Make the hands and feet by knotting the end of each arm and leg.

5 To make the parachute, roll the edges of the silk square and hem. You do not need to hem the edges if you are using a thin cotton handkerchief. Cut strong cotton yarn into lengths to create four equal strings, each 6 cm (2½ in) longer than the square.

6 Knot a string to each corner of the silk square, making sure the knots are secure, and trim the string ends. Fold the square in half to make sure that the strings are all the same length.

7 Attach the parachute to the person by knotting two strings to each arm. Make sure the knots are secure and trim.

Wind wands

As with many activities that involve the four elements of air, fire, earth and water, being out in nature enlivens all our senses. We feel the wind on our skin as a gentle touch, we listen to the different sounds made by leaves rustling in the trees, we see clouds drifting across the sky and smell the rain on the earth after a shower.

AWAKENING THE SENSES

A sudden breeze affects our sense of temperature; our sense of movement and balance are influenced as we are blown by a strong wind. Simply being in nature can enliven our whole sense of life.

Rudolf Steiner said that the world enters through the senses to nourish the spirit, and the spirit goes out to transform, to create the world anew. That is why it is important to provide a young child with an environment and experiences that nourish all the senses. Nature is one such environment and the more time spent in it, the better. Wind wands are great outdoor toys: providing a simple way of enjoying flying, they are the precursor to the more complicated kite-flying.

You can tie on different lengths or types of ribbon to add variety to the experience. For instance, strips of crêpe paper make a wonderful sound, crackling and rustling as they brush against each other. Satin ribbon, however, moves sleekly and fluidly, and the bright colours look wonderful when flying together in the wind.

A wind wand is made in such a way that your toddler can easily hold and shake it or, with big movements, swing it around in the air. Both you and your toddler can run down a hill together, each holding a wind wand. The more you can spend time outdoors playing with this type of toy with your young children, the more they will strengthen their limbs and enliven their senses.

Hints and tips
- Make sure you attach the ribbons securely to the circular wand.
- Opt for making the ribbons all the same colour, or choose colours that go well together or combine a number of different patterns.
- You can use coloured crêpe paper instead of ribbons, but make sure the crêpe does not get wet.

'Children cannot learn skills for handling the elements early enough… and for this, they must experience them first hand.'

Irmgard Kutsch and Brigitte Walden, *Nature Activities for Children*

Making a wind wand

These wind wands provide an airy activity that takes no skill at all
and can be enjoyed by children of all ages.

You will need

1 metre (40 in) thin cane

Strong thread

5 x 1 metre (40 in)
   lengths coloured ribbon

Dressmaking scissors

Sewing needle

Sewing thread

How to do it

1 Twist the cane into a neat hand-sized ring, weaving it in and out once or twice to keep its shape. Secure the ends with strong thread.

2 Hem what will be the loose end of each length of ribbon to prevent it fraying (or cut the ends at an angle).

3 Sew each length of ribbon onto the cane, spacing them evenly apart. Turn down each ribbon end before you sew it to the cane to prevent fraying.

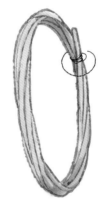

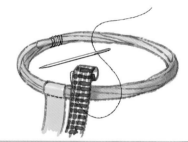

Rafts and boats

Water is particularly attractive for your young toddler. He spent nine months floating in liquid before birth and it seems natural for him to enjoy being in it afterwards. In the bath, he loves to splash and, once able to sit up, to play with anything that floats. Toddlers are drawn to puddles and happily splash in them when it's raining, never minding being wet or muddy.

PLAYING WITH WATER

Every child should have the opportunity to experience the outdoors in all weather, including in rain or snow. There should be no reason for avoiding colder days, as a young child is not yet conscious enough of his own body to be aware of sensations such as hot and cold, dry and wet. An old saying runs: 'There is no such thing as bad weather, just bad clothing!'. Dress your toddler for the occasion, with a hat to keep off the sun in summer and as protection from cold in winter, and with waterproof coveralls and boots in the rain. It is wise to put on layers of clothing in colder weather – you can always remove a layer. Your toddler will always need at least one layer more than you.

If properly dressed, a toddler can play for hours by a river or stream or at the seaside, damming up water or diverting it to flow in other directions. Always take care to be near young children when they are playing with water as they need constant supervision even if the water is shallow.

Hints and tips
- You could use garden cane instead of sticks.
- Make a small flag to attach to the end of each mast.
- Colour the sails or glue on pictures.

Playing with rafts and boats, however simple they are, is a way of finding out how the force of water can move an object. 'Pooh-sticks' is a great game that involves dropping different sizes of stick from one side of a bridge and running to the other side to see which is the fastest. Similarly, your child will love watching the way a stream carries a raft, moving it from eddy to eddy or down a rapid. She will delight in seeing a boat released from a pool where it might have stuck or simply floating it on a garden pond or even just in the bath.

A POND OF YOUR OWN

It is very easy to create your own little pond for floating rafts and boats outside. Simply take a wide, shallow basin and cover the base with gravel and nice stones and shells that you have collected with your toddler, before filling it with water. For added interest, put a vase of flowers or branches in one of the corners. Let your toddler watch as you guide the rafts and boats from one side to the other by blowing into the sails. He will discover how the power of breath – air – can move and direct a boat, and this is a wonderful way for him to practise blowing too. An older child might ask why the boats don't sink, but the toddler simply enjoys the process unquestioningly. If you want to play with the rafts and boats indoors, as part of floor play, you could use a blue cloth as the sea or a pond.

Making rafts and boats

Look for different types of wood from which to make these rafts and boats. Your toddler will find it interesting to experience their different qualities first-hand.

How to do it

1 To make a raft, cut a number of 8 cm (3¼ in) lengths from the seasoned sticks. You need enough to make a roughly 8 cm (3¼ in) square when laid side by side. Sand the sticks to remove any bumps.

2 Lay the sticks side by side. Cut two lengths of garden string and knot one around an end of the first stick. Wind the string under and around the end of each stick in turn to secure that side of the raft. Tie at a knot on the last stick. Knot the other length of string on the opposite end of the first stick and wind and tie up the other side of the raft in the same way.

3 Cut the lollipop sticks into approximately 8 cm (3¼ in) lengths and glue them in place over the string.

4 When the glue has set, drill a hole in the centre stick to fit the mast. Cut an 8 × 8 cm (3¼ × 3¼ in) sail from thin card and punch or cut holes in the middle of the top and bottom edges.

5 For the mast, cut an 8 cm (3¼ in) length from the thinner stick and thread it through both holes in the sail before gluing into the raft hole.

You will need

Straight seasoned sticks with a diameter of
 1 cm (½ in)

Saw

Sandpaper

Thin garden string

Sharp scissors

2 lollipop sticks

PVA glue

Drill and drill bits

Thin card

Slightly thinner straight seasoned stick

Piece of bark

6 To make a bark boat, cut a boat shape from a piece of bark. Cut a length from the thinner seasoned stick for the mast, about the same length as the boat.

7 Drill a hole in the bark hull for the mast. Use a drill bit that is slightly thinner than the mast and do not drill all the way through.

8 Cut a sail from thin card to fit the mast and glue it in position, leaving space at the bottom, underneath the sail.

9 Glue the mast into the drilled hole.

Felt balls

A ball is one of the first moving toys given to more active babies. We watch our babies' happiness when they discover how, in the simple exercise of giving a ball a little nudge, it moves of its own accord. Backwards and forwards we roll balls to our babies, toddlers and young children… a game of endless pleasure.

PLAYING BALL

You need to allow your toddler to play with objects, interact with other people and develop physical skills. Ball games provide an opportunity for all of these aspects. They can be very social activity, for playing ball with others is a non-threatening way of interaction, particularly during first contact with other children. When they are very young, they cannot throw or catch balls across a distance, although this skill develops as they grow and gain more physical control. Your toddler can also be left alone to see what a ball is capable of, bouncing it against a wall or rolling it into a bucket. No matter what children do with a ball, they will develop a range of physical skills and also discover what happens to a round object in different situations.

These soft balls are perfect for playing with outside and in. However, it is up to you to lay down the rules from the outset. 'We don't kick our ball or throw it high inside the house,' you can say. (Just make sure you stick to the rules!) Show your toddler how you can pass the ball gently to each other or roll it to and fro. Sit on the floor with your toddler, both with legs apart to catch the ball. You can use planks of wood to roll a ball from up high to down low or across a bridge with the plank propped on two chairs or blocks. This is a favourite of older toddlers in particular.

These balls have a simple design, are very easy to make and can be adapted to make balls of many sizes, colours and segments. For an older child, the balls will also provide an opportunity for colour recognition and counting the different segments.

Hints and tips

- A ball width is generally one-third the length of each segment, with about 2 mm (⅛ in) added for seams.
- Use a different colour felt for each segment or just two colours for alternate segments.
- Use contrasting embroidery thread.
- Sew a bell inside the ball before stuffing.
- For younger toddlers, sew a thread onto one end of a ball and tie it to the cot for bouncing.
- Attach ribbons or embroider with patterns or your child's name.

PLAYTIME

The following game can be enjoyed by any number of participants. Sit on the floor with legs stretched out and all feet touching to form a circle (or sit opposite each other if there are only two of you). Roll the ball from one person to the next singing a rhythmic song as you go. You can make up any tune to accompany the following words:

On and on the ball does wander
Now its here and now it's yonder,
Tell me quickly, one two three,
Where the rainbow ball will be.

See whose legs have caught the ball by the end of the rhyme. This provides an opportunity for the younger toddler to learn how to roll the ball and, as the skill is acquired, to roll it to a chosen person.

Making a felt ball

Instead of oversewing or using blanket stitch, you could use backstitch for a neater finish, sewing sections together, wrong sides out, then turning the ball right side out for stuffing.

You will need

Tracing paper

Pencil

Sturdy felt in different colours

Pins

Dressmaking scissors

Embroidery needle

Embroidery thread of different colours

Carded, unspun sheep's wool*

Pins

* Tease unspun sheep's wool before use, pulling gently to separate dense fibres. A comb-like hand 'carder' speeds up the process.

How to do it

1 To make a template for a four-segment ball, fold a piece of paper and mark a length of 11 cm (4½ in) along the fold. Now refold widthways and mark a width of 6 cm (2½ in). Draw from mark to mark to create the outline shown below. For a seven-segment ball, measure 12 cm (5 in) x 4.5 cm (1¾ in) or, for a smaller version, 9 cm (3½ in) x 3 cm (1¼ in). The illustrations below are drawn to scale and can be enlarged using a photocopier (it's best to make them at least as large as the measurements suggested above). Cut out your template and trim a few millimetres off each tip, as indicated. Pin the template to the felt and cut out the required number of sections.

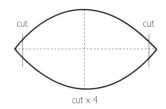

cut   cut

cut x 4

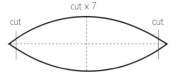

cut x 7

cut   cut

2 To make circular ends, cut out two felt circles in contrasting colours, about 2–4 cm (1–1½ in) in diameter depending on the size of ball. Square ends should measure about 2.5–3.5 cm (1–1½ in) on each side.

3 Oversew or blanket stitch (see pages 39 and 28) the sections together lengthways, using embroidery thread in a contrasting colour. Leave a small opening on the last section for stuffing.

4 Stuff the ball with unspun sheep's wool, making sure the shape is firm and round.

5 Pin on the ends, oversew them in place, then remove the pins. If you need to adjust the ball size, sew some gathering stitches around the top and bottom openings and pull tighter before sewing on the ends.

Tumbling men

It is fascinating to watch these roly-poly men tumble head over heels down a slope. Will they go in a straight line or turn corners? Will one man tumble faster than another? This is a toy of endless discovery. It is a perfect way for your child to orient himself in space, finding out where up and down and left and right are, and developing his sense of balance.

This is a good toy to have if your toddler is ill in bed or stuck inside on a rainy day. It is also small enough for you to carry in your pocket on an outing and bring out to play with when your little one needs occupying for a moment or two. You can also use it for a more sophisticated activity, building complicated surfaces for the men to roll down. Once you have put some of these ideas into practice, you can leave your toddler to play, on his own or with others, racing the little men down a cushion or ramp.

DEVELOPING SKILLS THROUGH PLAY
Active toys like these require some control from your toddler as he will need to balance the man and line him up straight at the top of the hill before letting go. If you make more than one tumbling man, in different sizes, your toddler will discover that the larger ones take longer to get to the bottom. If the cushion isn't straight, he will see how they roll to one side and even off the edge.

You can provide another dimension to the play by making tumbling men in different colours. Your toddler can use them as colourful circus clowns during floor play or race them with other children or with you. You can race them forwards or backwards down the ramp, depending on how you position them. Try starting them on their heads, propelling them off with a little push to their legs, or from a sitting position with a push to the back.

Hints and tips
- Try making tumbling girls or boys, or even little men with beards.
- To curl card, pull a length over the edge of a table, then roll to size and secure with sticking tape.
- Use strong glue.
- The best tumbling surface is not a smooth one; use a plank covered in fabric, a blanket or a cushion.

'The faculty of play becomes the origin and source of the most important skills and abilities we can develop in life.'

Martin Rawson, *Free Your Child's True Potential*

Making tumbling men

Make sure you secure the hats of these men well to stop the ball bearing or marble from escaping. It would be very tempting for a toddler to pop it straight into his mouth!

How to do it

You will need

Tracing paper

Pencil

Felt in different colours

Pins

Dressmaking scissors

Thin card

Sticking tape

PVA glue

Sewing needle

Sewing thread

Marble or ball bearing

Pencil crayons

1 Make paper templates for the jacket, trousers and hands by using a photocopier to enlarge the illustrations shown below to the desired size, or by drawing templates yourself. For a larger tumbling man, the jacket template should be about 8 cm (3¼ in) x 4 cm (1½ in), and the trousers about 7 cm (3 in) in length. A smaller jacket should be 7 cm (3 in) x 2.5 cm (1 in) and the trousers 6 cm (2½ in) long. Fold the felt in half, pin the templates along the fold as indicated in the illustration by a dotted line and cut out one jacket piece, one trouser piece and two hands for each man.

2 To make a head, roll a length of thin card into a tube of the desired size and secure with tape. For the large tumbling man described above, the head should be about 4 cm (1½ in) deep, with a diameter of

2.5 cm (1 in). A small head should be 3 cm (1¼ in) deep with a diameter of 2 cm (¾ in).

3 Cut a strip of face-coloured felt to fit around the head tube, leaving a gap of 5 mm (¼ in) at the top of the head tube. Glue the felt in place.

4 Cut a 2 cm (¾ in) slit in the middle of the jacket fold and push the bottom edge of the face tube through this hole. Make sure the face strip seam is at the back of the head and the gap is at the top of the tube.

5 Glue the inside surface of the circular jacket section. Position the trousers and two hands, then fold the body section in half over them and press firmly to stick.

6 Sew along the sealed edge of the jacket, from one hand to the other, stitching through both sides including hands and legs.

7 Place the marble or ball bearing inside the head tube. For the hat, cut a felt circle 1 cm (½ in) wider than the diameter of the tube Glue around the outside top edge of the tube, position the circle of felt over the top of the tube and press down the edges firmly to cover the opening.

8 Now glue a strip of contrasting felt, about 1 cm (½ in) x 8 cm (3¼ in) around the hat as a hat band. This will cover the join between face and hat and ensure it is secure enough to keep the marble or ball bearing in place. Position the seam at the back.

9 Finally, draw features on the face with coloured pencil crayons.

Butterfly mobile

This lovely mobile appeals to everyone who sees it, whether a baby, a toddler, a young child or an adult. It embodies colour, movement and sound and casts different impressions as it catches the sunlight, brightening up a dull corner of the kitchen or bedroom.

Use all the colours of the rainbow to make the butterflies or change their colours to reflect those of the changing seasons: green and yellow in summer and silver and red in winter. Make the mobile with your little one watching. It is so simple to make that she can join in and will enjoy twisting the pipe cleaner into a body, head and feelers or scrunching the tissue wings to fit into the body.

A CHILD'S ENVIRONMENT

You now know that the young child is deeply connected to the impressions made on her by her surroundings, be they the pure sounds she hears, the beauty she sees or the natural materials she touches. Rudolf Steiner talks of 12 distinct senses, many of which have been mentioned in this book.

As the child, because of her openness, is educated and formed by her environment and everything that takes place within it, it is of vital importance that the quality of her sensory experiences are carefully nurtured too. A young child's environment should be calm, peaceful and uncluttered and this includes everything from her clothing to the furnishings of her room. A few simple, aesthetically pleasing decorations are all that are required.

BUILDING A NATURE CORNER

A nature corner is a good way of adding decoration to a child's environment. This can be a small area – a windowsill, a small table or a shelf – dedicated to objects that represent each of the four elements. These might include a vase with branches or flowers, some shells in a bowl of water or collected stones of various colours. Focus on items you can collect outdoors together. Cover the surface with a coloured cloth and change it to suit the seasons.

It is important, as with everything else in your toddler's environment, to take care of this table and all the treasures displayed on it. Flowers will need clean water to drink and other items may need changing as they decay. Keep it simple – too many items and the senses become overburdened.

Hang the butterfly mobile from the ceiling above your nature corner so that it can float and flutter in the breeze or twirl round gently driven by the current caused by the heat of a candle.

Hints and tips

- If you want to colour your pipe cleaners, do so with paint or pencil crayons.
- For greater interest, hang the butterflies at different levels.
- Suspend the mobile near a window so that it catches the breeze.
- When the tissue paper colours begin to fade, or the mobile becomes dusty, replace it with a new one.

Making a butterfly mobile

If making a large number of butterflies, try to hang them as straight as you can to prevent them from knocking into one another and getting into a tangle.

How to do it

You will need

Flexible cane

Coloured ribbon

Sharp scissors

Tissue paper

Pipe cleaners

Sewing thread

1 Decide on the diameter of your mobile and wind the cane into a ring, weaving it in and out a couple times to secure. Tuck in the ends.

2 Wind a length of coloured ribbon around the ring for decoration.

3 Attach four equal-length ribbons to the cane ring, making sure they are evenly spaced and hang level. Tie the loose ends together, then attach another ribbon to the four so that you can hang the mobile centrally from the single ribbon.

4 To make the butterflies, cut shapes from folded tissue paper to make sure they are symmetrical. Layer the paper so that you cut several butterflies at a time.

5 Choosing different colours, layer two or three butterfly shapes on top of each other. Fold a pipe cleaner in half and pinch the tissue paper between the two halves, scrunching the paper gently to give the butterfly form.

6 Twist the ends of the pipe cleaner to secure the tissue paper and bend the ends to form the head and feelers.

7 Fluff up the wings, then tie a length of sewing thread to each end of the pipe cleaner. Attach a second piece of thread to the first and knot so that it can slide up and down the first thread until the butterfly hangs straight.

8 Attach the butterflies to the cane ring, making sure they are evenly spaced and hang at different lengths.

Index

Further reading

Aeppli, Willi and Freilich, Elizabeth, *Care and Development of the Human Senses*, Steiner Schools Fellowship Publications, Forest Row, new edition 1993

Baldwin, Rahima Dancy, *You are Your Child's First Teacher*, Hawthorn Press, Stroud, 2006

Bettelheim, Bruno, *The Uses of Enchantment: The meaning and importance of fairy tales*, Thames & Hudson, London, 1976

Callois, Roger, *Man, Play and Games*, Free Press of Glencoe, New York, 1961

Clouder, Christopher and Nicol, Janni, *Creative Play for your Baby: Steiner Waldorf expertise and toy projects for 3 months–2 years*, Gaia, London, 2007

Clouder, Christopher and Rawson, Martyn, *Waldorf Education: Rudolf Steiner's ideas in practice*, Floris Books, Edinburgh, 2003

Cohen, David, *The Development of Play*, Routledge, London, 1996

Florida, Richard and Tinagli, Irene, *Europe in the Creative Age*, Demos, London, 2004

Froebel Friedrich, *The Pedagogics of the Kindergarten: Ideas concerning the play and playthings of the child*, University Press of the Pacific, Honolulu, new edition 2003

Gallahue, David L, and Ozmun, John, C., *Understanding Motor Development: Infants, children, adolescents, adults*, McGraw-Hill, Boston, 1998

Garvey, Catherine, *Play (Developing Child)*, Fontana, London, 1991

Ginnsberg, Kenneth, R. and the Committee on Communications and the Committee on Psychosocial Aspects of Child and Family Health, 'The Importance of Play in Promoting Healthy Child Development and Maintaining Strong Parent–Child Bonds', *Pediatrics*, vol. 119, no. 1, American Academy of Pediatrics, January 2007

Glöckler, Michaela and Goebel, Wolfgang, *A Guide to Child Health*, Floris Books, Edinburgh, 2003

Huizinga, Johan, *Homo Ludens: A study of the play-element in culture*, Beacon Press, Boston, 1971

Kutsch, Irmgard and Walden, Brigitte, *Nature Activities for Children*, Floris Books, Edinburgh, 2007

Layard, Richard, *Happiness: Lessons from a new science*, Penguin, London, 2006

Liedloff, Jean, *The Continuum Concept*, Penguin, London, 1989

Male, Dot, *The Parent and Child Group Handbook: A Steiner/Waldorf approach*, Hawthorn Press, Stroud, 2005

Mehler, Jacques and Dupoux, Emmanuel, *What Infants Know: The new cognitive science of early development*, Blackwell, Oxford, 1993

Montessori, Maria, *The Absorbent Mind*, ABC-CLIO, Oxford, new edition 1988

Montessori, Maria, *The Advanced Montessori Method: Her programme for educating elementary school children vol. 1*, ABC-CLIO, Oxford, new edition 1991

Moss, Peter and Penn, Helen, *Transforming Nursery Education*, Paul Chapman Publishing, London, 1996

Neill, A.S., *Summerhill School*, Saint Martin's Press, New York, St Martin's Griffin edition 1998

Palmer, Sue, *Toxic Childhood: How the modern world is damaging our children and what we can do about it*, Orion Books, London, 2006

Pearce, Joseph Chilton, *Evolution's End: Claiming the potential of our intelligence*, Harper Collins, San Francisco, 1992

Pearce, Joseph Chilton, *Magical Child*, Penguin, reprinted 1992

Rawson, Martin, *Free Your Child's True Potential*, Hodder and Stoughton, London, 2001

Rogoff, Barbara, *Apprenticeship in Thinking: Cognitive development in social context*, Oxford University Press, Oxford, 1990

Santer, Joan, Griffiths, Carol and Goodall, Deborah, *Free Play in Early Childhood: A literature review*, National Children's Bureau, London, 2007

Schiller, Friedrich, *On the Aesthetic Education of Man: In a series of letters*, Oxford University Press, Oxford, reprinted 1983

Selleck, D, 'Being under Three Years of Age: Enhancing quality experiences' in G. Pugh, *Contemporary Issues in the Early Years*, Paul Chapman Publishing, London, 2001

Steiner, Rudolf and Harwood, A.C., *Study of Man: General education course*, Steiner Press, London, new edition 2004

Steiner, Rudolf, *The Child's Changing Consciousness and Waldorf Education*, Rudolf Steiner Press, Forest Row, new edition 1988

Steiner, Rudolf, *The Kingdom of Childhood: Foundations of Waldorf education*, Steiner Books/Anthroposophic Press, Great Barrington, new edition 1995

Steiner, Rudolf, *The Roots of Education*, Rudolf Steiner Press, Forest Row, new edition 1998

Steiner, Rudolf, *The World of the Sense and the World of the Spirit*, Steiner Books/Anthroposophic Press, New Barrington, new edition 1979

Steiner, Rudolf, *Understanding Young Children: Extracts from lectures*, International Association of Waldorf Kindergartens, Stuttgart, 1975

Steiner, Rudolf, Wegman, Ita and Meuss, A.R., *Extending Practical Medicine: Fundamental Principles Based on the Science of the Spirit*, Rudolf Steiner Press, Forest Row, new edition 2000

Tower R.B. and Singer J.L., 'Imagination, Interest and Joy in Early Childhood' in P.E. McGhee and A.J. Chapman (eds), *Children's Humour*, John Wiley, Hoboken, 1980

Wood, Elizabeth and Attfield, Jane, *Play, Learning and the Early Childhood Curriculum*, Paul Chapman Publishing, 1996

Woodhead, Martin, Faulkner, Dorothy and Littleton, Karen (eds), *Cultural Worlds of Early Childhood: Child development in families, schools and societies*, Routledge, London, 1998

Zahlingen, Bronja, *A Lifetime of Joy*, WECAN Books, Spring Valley, 2005

Find out more about the Alliance for Childhood at www.allianceforchildhood.org.uk.

Acknowledgements

Author acknowledgements
We would like to thank those who deliberately and inadvertently gave us help, inspiration and advice, colleagues, parents and children alike.

Photographic acknowledgements
Special Photography © Octopus Publishing Group Limited/Mike Prior

Publisher acknowledgements
The publisher would like to thank Janni Nicol for making the toys for this book, with the help and encouragement of her husband Simon. Thanks to Fiona White for making the standing puppets, marionettes and wind wands. Thanks also to all the children who were photographed for this book (and their parents and guardians for bringing them along): Ariele Long, Ava Hubbard, Betty McDonald, Caitlin Smith, Cyrus Couchman-Kosir, Eva Lykourgiotis, Lola Sedelmeier, Maia Solomon, Matthew Ellis, Oliver Reynolds, Owen William Davies, Rima Couchman-Kosir, Robert James, Rosie James, Theo Solomon, Ziggy Aplin.

Every reasonable effort has been made to trace copyright holders of the extracts reproduced in this book. The publisher apologizes for any errors or omissions and would be grateful if notified of any corrections that should be incorporated in future reprints or editions of this book. Extracts have been reproduced by kind permission of the following publishers:
p.9: From *Extending Practical Medicine* by Rudolf Steiner, Ita Wegman and A.R. Meuss, Rudolf Steiner Press, Forest Row, 2000
p.21: From *You are Your Child's First Teacher* by Rahima Baldwin Dancy, Ten Speed Press, Berkeley, 2000 and Hawthorn Press, Stroud, 2006
p.25: From *The Child's Changing Consciousness and Waldorf Education* by Rudolf Steiner, Rudolf Steiner Press, Forest Row, 1988
p.42: From *Homo Ludens* by Johan Huizinga. Copyright © 1950 by Roy Publishers. Reprinted by permission of Beacon Press, Boston
p.42: From *The Uses of Enchantment* by Bruno Bettelheim. Copyright © 1975, 1976 by Bruno Bettelheim. First published in the UK in 1976 by Thames & Hudson Ltd, London and in the USA and Canada by Aldred Knopf Inc.
p.44: From *The Kingdom of Childhood* by Rudolf Steiner, Steiner Books/Anthroposophic Press, Great Barrington, 1995
p.55: From *The Roots of Education* by Rudolf Steiner, Rudolf Steiner Press, Forest Row, 1998
p.81: From *A Lifetime of Joy* by Bronja Zahlingen, Waldorf Early Childhood Association of North American (WECAN) Books, Spring Valley, 2005
p.93: Extract by Joseph Chilton Pearce taken from www.ttfuture.org by kind permission of Michael Mendizza
p.98: From *The World of the Sense and the World of the Spirit* by Rudolf Steiner, Steiner Books/Anthroposophic Press, New Barrington, 1979
p.106: By kind permission of Floris Books. From *Nature Activities for Children* by Irmgard Kutsch and Brigitte Walden, Floris Books, Edinburgh, 2007

Executive editor Jessica Cowie
Senior editor Fiona Robertson
Executive art editor Leigh Jones
Designer Jo Tapper
Illustrator Kate Simunek
Senior production controller Simone Nauerth
Toymaker Janni Nicol